Making Acupuncture Pay

Real-World Advice for Successful Private Practice

By

Matthew D. Bauer, L.Ac.

First published by Dog Ear Publishing
4010 W. 86th Street, Ste H
Indianapolis, IN 46268
www.dogearpublishing.net

ISBN: 978-145750-279-8

This book is printed on acid-free paper.

Printed in the United States of America

Dedication

I dedicate this book to my Mother.
Momma – knowing you were always there made it all OK. I love you.

CONTENTS

Acknowledgments:

Several people helped provide very useful advice that no doubt made this a better book. I sought this feedback from those with a lot of experience treating large numbers of patients, those with moderate experience struggling to build practices, and also students or recent graduates just starting-out. Pamela R. Howard, M.A., M.Ac., L.Ac., Vlasta Fencl, L.Ac., Brent Ottley, L.Ac., Lisa Rohleder, L.Ac., and Irwin Tjiong, L.Ac., all gave me insightful suggestions that I used in my many re-writes and that found their way into the final draft. I owe a special thank to Lisa Rohleder who told me I needed to do what I could to share my experience with others. Lisa, more than anyone or anything helped me to realize my practice and practice model was the exception rather than the rule and that got me thinking about writing it down. Both Lisa and Robert Doane, L.Ac., also generously gave me their OK regarding my description of their practice models.

My son, Bryce Bauer, was instrumental in all aspects of editing this material. He is a gifted writer and editor and he saved me from some embarrassingly bad ideas—book ideas anyway. My wife Gayle, as always, was helpful in more ways than I can fully appreciate.

And I of course must acknowledge my many teachers and patients. The knowledge of my teachers has been passed through me to the benefit of my patients while the lessons learned from my patients I attempt to pass along here for the benefit of my readers.

CHAPTER ONE

Introduction, Housekeeping, and a Journeyman Acupuncturist

I decided to write this book as I approached my twenty-fifth year in practice. Twenty-five years. It's hard to believe. Time flew. I never became rich and I cannot yet afford to retire. I suspect I will need to continue to practice at some level into my seventies which is fine with me because I love what I do. While my many years of practice has not allowed me to stroll down "Easy Street", I have long considered myself blessed to have had the success I have had—success both in being able to support my family in a comfortable manner and in helping most of the thousands of patients who sought my help.

My decision to write this book, however, was not based on some nostalgic notion of sharing my experiences to celebrate my practice's silver anniversary but rather the realization that my level of success is not at all common in the Licensed Acupuncturist profession. I had long known that some acupuncturists struggled to make it in private practice but what I did not realize until recently is how bad this situation actually is. While statistics are scarce, the few that are out there show some serious problems.

The National Certification Commission for Acupuncture and Oriental Medicine's 2008 Job Training Analysis of NCCAOM Diplomats found that 88% of those who responded to that survey were in solo private practice and their average annual gross income was between $41,000 to $60,000 per year. 70.1% grossed under $61,000, 21.1% grossed between $61,000 to $120,000, and just 8.8% grossed over $121,000. The important thing to remember about these statistics is that when you are in solo private practice, a large chunk of your gross income—at least 30% to 40% and maybe more—is eaten-up by expenses such as rent, utilities, advertising, supplies, insurance, etc. When you subtract those expenses of doing business from the gross income, this brings the average before tax income of nearly three out of four Licensed Acupuncturists to no better than $30,000 to $40,000 a year. When you then subtract the additional self-employment taxes one has when self-employed and realize that this income does not include any health insurance or retirement benefits, you see that these are dismal figures. It is hard to imagine supporting a family and enjoying a comfortable living on those wages especially considering that 50% of those surveyed were carrying an average of more than $40,000 in student loans. What we still don't know is how many acupuncturists go out of business after a few years of struggling although some estimate that percentage to be upwards to 50%! I hope it is not that high but I am afraid it might be.

I find the above statistics to be a tragedy and completely unacceptable, especially considering how valuable and necessary the skills of a Licensed Acupuncturist are in our society. There is simply no good reason why people trained with these skills should be struggling to make a comfortable living. There are obviously problems with the preparation of those entering this profession that is keeping those with badly needed skills from earning the type of income those skills warrant. I wanted to write this book because I believed I could help those entering this field better prepare themselves for successful practice.

In offering my advice, I am not suggesting that I have all the answers or that everyone should try to duplicate what I have done in my own career. I do, however, have an unusual mixture of experience of building a successful practice from scratch, maintaining it as my family's source of income for more than 20 years, and staying abreast of many developments in the evolution of the Licensed Acupuncturist profession. I have also worked for nearly 15 years as a consultant for an insurance company, helping create and oversee utilization management and credentialing policies for acupuncture HMO plans and as an expert witness both in private cases and for the State of California. These experiences have helped me gain insights concerning a broad range of issues relating to the acupuncture/Oriental medicine (A/OM) profession.

Some of what I have to say about building a practice might conflict with what you thought or have been taught about earning a living in this field. I think it is essential however, that someone who has made their living via their practice and kept current with the profession gives it to you straight. I will be offering my critique on where I think our profession has been falling short and how those trying to enter this field may be unrealistic in their expectations but I am not being critical for the sake of being critical. The recent statistics show us that some significant adjustments are needed within this profession and I am trying to offer insights gained from my years of experience in the hope this will help others experience the success I have been privileged to enjoy.

I had originally thought of titling this book *How to Achieve the Blessing of Earning a Comfortable Living While Helping Others* because that is the way I look at this line of work; being able to make a nice living and support a family while helping others is truly a rare blessing. Achieving this blessing is worth all the effort it takes to make it happen. So while this book is designed to offer you the advice you need to succeed in practice, the underlying philosophy I suggest you follow is that you are working to achieve the rare blessing of making a comfortable living while helping others. Acupuncturists are in the business of helping others. Private practice is a business and you do need to learn how to manage business realities, but you also need to balance the business issues with the goal of helping your patients as best you can. I thought of many possible titles. I settled on *Making Acupuncture Pay* even though this book is not primarily about making money because acupuncturists should not shy away from the fact that their practices need to be financially successful in order for them to have the opportunity to help others.

Getting good clinical results are necessary to build a successful practice and that subject is an essential part of this book also but this is not a book advocating a particular treatment technique as the "best" method to treat such-and-such conditions. There are plenty of teachers out there teaching their techniques to treat specific conditions and sifting through the overwhelming number of options to find what techniques suit your own strengths is a personal struggle all acupuncturists must go through. This book is meant to help you get the most out of whatever particular style of treatment you prefer by focusing on the many real-world considerations an acupuncturist working in private practice must understand to be successful. I will offer some of my favorite point combinations for treating common conditions, but the focus here will be on the unique realities of a private practice setting rather than details of particular techniques.

Building a successful acupuncture practice requires making some tough choices such as where to locate your practice, how much to charge, etc. Writing a book on practice building also calls for making some tough choices. I chose to focus on acupuncture and not cover herbs or other services often associated with an acupuncture practice because acupuncture is what got this healing system's foot in the door in the West and continues to be the practice that captures the public's attention more than any other. I also chose to target students and those in their first years of practice rather than those with established practices because I felt it was important for someone to emphasize how vital it is to start a practice the right way. Of course, I hope those in established practices and those using herbs will also find my advice of value. I am using the abbreviation A/OM for "acupuncture/Oriental medicine." I chose to put the "/" between "acupuncture" and "Oriental medicine" signifying "acupuncture or acupuncture and Oriental Medicine" because some practitioners only practice acupuncture and not the broader system of Oriental medicine while others practice multiple techniques. And finally, I am using "Oriental medicine" because so many of the organizations that make-up the A/OM infrastructure use that term. I hope one day we will settle on a title or term everyone will agree upon.

I included the introduction as part of Chapter One because I feel it helps put the materials that follow into perspective and some readers skip the introduction. For those skippers who like to jump to the meat of things on the first read, you could begin at Chapter Four after finishing this chapter. Chapter Two explains why private practice is all that awaits most entering the A/OM profession and Chapter Three gives details of my first years in practice. I included chapter recaps at the ends of Chapters 7-15 because they contain the most detailed advice about how to manage patients and I thought recaps would make that more dense material easier to learn. I tried to avoid getting too cute with chapter titles so you should be able to find the subject matter you are looking for by those titles.

While I did my best to make this book a helpful guide to successful practice, I don't think any book by itself can offer all the help some may need to help them launch a new career. To address this, I have decided to do what I can over the next few years to help in this regard and this book is just one part of the efforts I expect to make. Many practitioners need more personalized help and I will be working on additional resources to address this. To that end, I will be developing additional training resources to expand on the information in this book, such as CEU/PDA offerings including live classes and web-based methods for practitioners who seek more detailed information and advice. I am not a tech-savvy guy so please bear with me as I try to figure out the best ways to take advantage of the web-based methods. As you will be learning throughout this book, one of my keys to practice building is learning how to give quality service at rates that are affordable. I learned how to do this in my practice and I will be learning how to do the same in the practice-building resources I plan to develop. I believe the web-based methods should offer the most cost-effective means to do so although I also look forward to live teaching opportunities when feasible. To learn more about these additional resources please visit my website at: www.MakingAcupuncturePay.com

A Journeyman Acupuncturist

Before beginning my A/OM schooling, I had completed apprenticeships in two different construction trades. They were both two-year apprenticeships that involved going through six stages of different pay scales. You began the training at 40% of a journeyman's pay and every four months your pay went up by 10%. In my case, events took place that didn't allow me to get the full training I should have had by the time I "turned-out" as a journeyman. This meant I had to work extra hard to make-up for my lack of training to justify my pay. After changing careers and completing my A/OM training, I immediately opened my practice and felt once again that I was under-trained and needed to work extra hard in order to survive in practice and support my family.

In the construction trades, a journeyman is someone who has the knowledge and experience to solve most any problem that gets thrown their way. They may make mistakes and not be as good at accomplishing some jobs as others, but give them some time and they can figure out how to get the job done or know when they need specialized help. Sometime into my second or third year of practice after having a week of seeing several patients with a wide assortment of different problems, it struck me that I had finally become a "journeyman" acupuncturist—able to provide a competent service to most anyone who walked in my door no matter what kinds of problems they had. That's pretty darn cool and why I love this work.

Feeling that I had become a journeyman acupuncturist was great (and still is) but that achievement alone was not what was responsible for the growth of my practice. Having the clinical skills to help people in theory and being able to do so while earning a living in private practice are two different things. My father was legendary as one of the most skilled workers in his construction trade as a Union worker for hire. But when he tried to strike-out on his own as a contractor, he failed and ended-up going back to Union work owing a lot of money. As skilled as he was in his trade, he did not have great business skills as a self-employed contractor. There are many clinically qualified A/OM practitioners who similarly struggle or fail in their practices because they don't understand how to translate their clinical abilities into a viable self-employed business. My father had the option to be a worker for hire or self-employed. At this point in time the worker for hire option is virtually non-existent for A/OM practitioners as I will detail in the next chapter. For the vast majority of those entering the A/ OM profession, making a living means one needs to be successful in private practice and that takes knowledge in subjects beyond diagnosis and treatment.

In addition to achieving journeyman clinical abilities, you need "Business 101" knowledge like how to set budgets and manage finances. You also need an understanding of basic medical private practice issues like patient recordkeeping and insurance billing. Most A/OM students will get at least a little training in those two areas and there are other resources available that address these subjects as well. But beyond the basic business and medical private practice subjects, there are a host of skills needed that are unique to managing a private A/OM practice in the West. These are abilities that span the business and clinical aspects and these subjects are almost never identified or even discussed in the A/OM profession. On one hand, you could say that it only takes two primary skills to build a successful A/OM practice: You must get prospective patients in your door and then make sure they go out that door satisfied with your services. The problem is that each of these two requires competence in many unique sub-skills and the training received in school typically only addresses a portion of the knowledge needed. The goal of this book is to identify and offer practical advice on those skill sets unique to managing an A/OM practice in the West today. I also hope doing so will further discussion of practice building issues within the A/OM profession.

The services offered in an A/OM practice are not at all well understood by those we seek to service. That's a big problem. You need to be able to appreciate this lack of understanding and have the means to address this. You also need to have a keen awareness of the anxiety many people have about seeking-out acupuncture and I am not just referring to the fear of needles. The public has no understanding of what to expect when they consult an acupuncturist and they don't understand how acupuncture works therapeutically. Then, there is the issue of cost. How do you structure your fees to make it affordable for your patients to get the treatments they need and allow you to earn a living? How should you space the treatments over what period of time? All of these factors and many more will have a great impact on how you manage your business as a private practitioner.

As I went through the process of writing this book I thought of the construction apprenticeship pay scales and how they relate to the training needed to succeed in practice. Using this model as a means to put this issue in perspective, I would say that most graduates of our A/OM schools receive training at a 70% apprenticeship level at best in clinical skills and no better than 30% or 40% in the unique skills of marketing and managing a private A/OM practice. It may not be possible for our schools to train graduates at full journeyman level in all the skills required to succeed in practice and that leaves those entering this profession needing additional resources to help them identify and fill-in the gaps in their training.

It is only natural that schools will focus most of their attention on attaining and maintaining accreditation and high licensing exam pass rates and I don't wish to be too critical, especially as I have never worked in any school management position. However, if you look at where most of the A/OM schools are at in this stage of our profession's development, it seems that very few students attending our schools get much training from those who have actually made their living in private practice. Some of our best teachers developed their clinical expertise working in the Far East under socialized medical systems or as employees within hospitals or large clinics. While the high volume of patients and hospital privileges such systems generate afforded these practitioners tremendous clinical experience, this style of practice is far removed from running a private acupuncture practice in the West.

The same is true for the school clinics in which most students get their hands-on training. While many of these clinics have some first-rate clinical teachers, the multi-practitioner, school-owned teaching clinic is also very different from private practice, especially solo private practice. Some schools will have arrangements with private practitioners allowing students to get training in a private practice setting. This can be helpful because it is much closer to the manner most students will end up practicing themselves, but often these arrangements don't allow for students to follow specific patients through the entire treatment process—knowledge critical to patient management. Also, this type of training usually does not involve the business side of private practice. Considering the above, most acupuncture students get very little exposure to the realities of earning one's living from solo private practice despite the recent evidence that this is where nearly nine out of ten of them end-up. No wonder graduates struggle once they "turn-out" as licensed practitioners.

One could even go so far as to say that the A/OM profession in the U.S. and probably the West in general got off on the wrong foot as far as business models go. We initially needed to import most of our teachers from cultures that deliver A/OM services in completely different settings and we were so focused on developing our clinical knowledge that we overlooked the market realities within which that knowledge would be applied.

Although acupuncture is now experiencing an explosion of worldwide growth, during the first half of the 20th Century it had actually reached its lowest point in its more than 2,000 year history. China, Korea, and Japan all struggled greatly after the advent of the Western scientific and industrial revolutions. East Asian traditional practices, once a great source of pride within these cultures, became viewed as a backwards hindrance to needed progress and were largely unsupported by any institutions. It was only after the 1950's when China's Chairman Mao Tse-Tung decided to institutionalize traditional medicine as part of his government's health care system that acupuncture started to rebound.

I point this out to illustrate that while it is true that acupuncture has survived more than 2,000 years of continuous practice, we can't look back to its recent history to help us understand how it was best practiced from a practice model perspective. Acupuncture has gone from an almost disregarded ancient relic to being the superstar of the alternative medicine field in a mere 50 years. Its growth in clinical popularity has far outpaced the growth in the models employed to deliver its clinical benefit. Even in China today many acupuncturists are leaving that field because they cannot make a living off it. So, while we can all marvel at acupuncture's resiliency and applaud the fact that it is gaining worldwide recognition as a useful method of healthcare, much more progress is needed to understand how *acupuncturists* can actually make a living delivering that care.

What Is Acupuncture's Value?

Value: *Extent to which a good or service is perceived by its customer to meet his or her needs or wants, measured by customer's willingness to pay for it. It commonly depends more on the customer's perception of the worth of the product than on its intrinsic value.* businessdictionary.com Value; Marketing

After the NCCAOM's 2008 Job Training Analysis statistics were released, there started to be more discussion in the A/OM profession about why so many practitioners are struggling and failing in their practices. Some think the problem is a lack of education believing A/OM students need more and better education. Among those are some who say more education is needed in Western medicine and science so those entering the profession can better communicate with Western medicine specialists and become integrated into mainstream medicine. Others say the problem is that students don't learn their A/OM skills at a high enough level and so are not as successful with their patients as they could be. Still others say the problem lies with not learning the basic business skills of how to run a practice.

Others have criticized the fees many A/OM practitioners charge and the high costs of training and licensing as the greatest problem. They stress that high treatment fees place acupuncture out of reach for most working class people and have turned acupuncture into a kind of luxury for the upper classes. They also point out that high debt levels from student loans put those trying to start their practices so deeply in the hole that they can't claw their way out.

As for myself, I have long advocated that the main problem is a lack of public education or marketing. I have stressed that the public does not understand our services and the key to improving the success rate for practices is for both individual practitioners and the profession as a whole to undertake smart public education efforts.

Throughout the process of writing this book, I gave these theories including my own a great deal of thought. I now believe that while all of these theories have at least some merit, none alone capture the essence of the problem of how to make a living in this field. The reason I now feel this way stems from my realization that there are acupuncturists struggling all over the world who are doing so despite not having at least some of the problems listed above. For example, there are Medical Doctors who practice acupuncture and have no lack of education in Western medicine and science and are already integrated into mainstream medicine yet they cannot make acupuncture work financially in their practices. Some of these doctors have successful private medical practices and so their problem is not a lack of knowledge of how to run a private practice or student loan debt.

In China, as I mentioned earlier, acupuncture is mainly delivered at a very low cost, a fee set by the government of about sixty cents for a course of treatments. There, acupuncturists are leaving that field because they can't make a living being paid so little. These practitioners have extensive training in both Western and Chinese medical subjects, are integrated into their country's mainstream medical system, and, unlike in the West, the public has a fair understanding of their services.

So, if clinical education or high treatment fees or public education alone is not the problem, why are many acupuncturists all over the world struggling to make a reasonable living? I believe the problem lies with addressing how to establish the proper value of acupuncture services within whatever marketplace those services are being delivered. Acupuncture "can" be effective in a remarkably wide range of different medical conditions but the odds that a series of treatments "will" be successful for any given patient is difficult to know. The odds of success will vary depending on a complex dynamic of factors including the type of condition being treated, the level of training and experience of the practitioner, the number of treatments given over what period of time, the level of cooperation of the patient, and many more.

Not knowing the odds that a given number of treatments will prove just how successful for a given patient makes calculating the value of acupuncture very difficult. Not knowing the value of acupuncture makes setting charges for those services difficult to say the least. It also makes the question of educating practitioners—both the content and cost—hard to determine. Practitioners do need the clinical skills to get journeyman results for their patients. Fees do have to be affordable for patients while allowing enough for the practitioner to make a living. Patients and the public do need to understand just what acupuncture can do for them. Students do need to leave school with low enough debt to make a living while paying-off their education costs. Striking the right balance between all these factors is essential to making a living as an acupuncturist. Just how to strike that balance will vary depending on things like what country/culture is involved, what type of patient is being treated, what the income needs of the practitioner are, etc.

I don't know what advice to offer acupuncturists working in China about how to improve their situation. The same goes for acupuncturists in many other parts of the world. I don't have the first-hand experience with the dynamics of the specific factors that influence their struggles. I am not even sure I could offer insights to the Medical Doctors practicing acupuncture here in the West about how to make acupuncture work financially in their practices. Their overheads/income expectations may just be too high. I do believe, however, that I can help those coming out of acupuncture schools in the U.S. and perhaps other Western countries put the relevant factors into perspective and learn how to make a living practicing acupuncture.

Acupuncture is valuable and the value of acupuncture should absolutely allow for private practitioners to earn a reasonable living. The problem is learning how to manage the fact that assessing the value of acupuncture is so tricky. When you open a private practice, you are going into business as a self-employed, small business entrepreneur. Specifically, you are establishing a type of service business; providing a service for a fee. But let's think about this service business you are opening:

Unlike most service businesses, the outcomes of the services you will offer are difficult to predict and this will make it difficult for you to establish your fees. Contrast this with other services businesses. A house painter or hair stylist will be able to explain to you how much they charge and just what you will get for that price. There may be some uncertainty over how well the job gets done, but your house will have paint applied or your hair will get cut. When a patient comes to an acupuncturist, they do so for the service of getting relief for their problems, not just to get needles stuck in them. Unfortunately, neither the patient nor practitioner knows for sure if the patient's problem will be fixed or even helped at all. How do you set charges for providing a service when you can't be sure of the outcome of that service? How do you make a potential patient feel comfortable about engaging your services with this uncertainty hanging in the air?

If you knew just how much you could help a patient's problem over exactly how many treatments, you could set a price and it would be a simple matter for the patient to decide if they thought that service was worth the price. Then, your biggest challenge would be making the cost of your services competitive with others providing the same service. But an acupuncturist cannot have set prices for sciatica, headaches, allergies, and so forth, because we cannot be certain exactly how many treatments will be needed or even if any number of treatments will get the job done at all. That is a major problem that saps the confidence of many beginning acupuncturists. When patients who already have doubts and anxieties about you and your services pick-up on that lack of confidence, you've lost them.

Some might say that this same problem exists in any health care field—that there are no guarantees in the medicine. While that is true, it is far less a problem in most other health care businesses. Many doctors or therapists delivering Western medical services do so while being paid a salary within a hospital or large clinic setting where the majority of the payment for those services comes from third parties like HMO's or Medicare. Even those Western medical providers working within their own private practices still have most of the cost of their services paid for by third party payment. Having no or limited third party help with the cost of A/OM services greatly magnifies the stress involved with not being able to make any guarantees about the outcome. The public also understands how Western medical services are supposed to work in theory. They don't understand how sticking needles in people can help the range of different conditions acupuncturists claim.

All successful A/OM practitioners find ways to manage this stressful situation even without necessarily realizing they are doing so. I developed my methods for managing this by trial and error over years of building my practice but I never took the time to identify this as a key to my success until I wrote this book. Had anyone told me when I first opened my practice that this was the biggest problem I must learn to manage to be successful it would have made my first years in practice go much easier. As the inability to effectively manage this issue may well be the biggest reason A/OM practices struggle or even fail, I am excited to share with you the system I developed to manage this.

What I will be teaching you is how to establish a service business delivering a no-guarantee medical service whose value is difficult to determine and has limited third party payment support and to do so for a public that does not understand how your services work and has little if any respect for your training. While that may sound like an impossible task, the good news is that it can be done once you address how to value acupuncture services within your market. While I will be offering advice on basic business and private medical practice subjects, most of the focus will be on how to manage delivering a service that is difficult to value and that the public does not understand. Here are some of the key concepts I will be teaching you in this regard:

How to estimate the odds of success – There is a logical system for determining the odds of treatment success that will allow you to explain this to your patients up front and also deepen your own understanding of the strengths and limits of your therapies.

How to communicate with patients and potential patients – Making acupuncture easily understandable without confusing jargon plays a big role in practice building. The explanations I will teach you will make this so simple you'll wonder why no one ever taught this to you before.

How to squeeze the most from the least – Learning how to help your patients more effectively with fewer treatments will increase the value of those treatments in your patient's eyes.

How to space your treatments and why – Daily, weekly, monthly? Knowing this is as important as any diagnostic skill or treatment technique and is critical to squeezing more from less.

How to determine your fee structure – You might have great technique but if no one can afford your services, your technique ends up doing no one any good.

First Survive, Then Thrive

As we consider how to make your service business (practice) successful, special attention must be paid to surviving the first few years while laying a firm foundation for future growth. Most businesses that fail do so within the first few years. While most all practices will continue to need to attract new patients as the years go by, this becomes less of a problem the longer a practice has survived (if the patients were happy with the service provided). The more patients you treat over the longer period of time, the more repeat patients you will have and the more referrals your patients will provide. Building an existing practice to higher patient volumes or higher profitability (those two are not always one and the same) becomes easier the longer a practice has been successfully operating. That is why so much focus needs to be placed on surviving and building sound habits in how you run your practice. Doing so has allowed my practice to continue to grow even through the current Great Recession.

Considering how important it is to survive those first years, one might think that the first of the two primary skills I mentioned above—attracting potential patients (marketing) is the most crucial to focus on. While it is important to work on getting potential patients in your door, the second primary skill of making sure they go out that door satisfied with your services (patient satisfaction) is even more important. Why? Because nothing will kill a young practice faster than unhappy patients. If you go to a new restaurant and the food or service was bad, chances are you will not go back and you will tell all your friends to stay away. While I will be referring from this point onward to "patient satisfaction" or "satisfaction rates", what I really mean about the need to achieve high patient satisfaction rates is that there is a need to have very low patient *dissatisfaction* rates. You really don't want a flood of new patients if you have not yet learned how to achieve high satisfaction/low dissatisfaction rates. Satisfied initial patients are both the key to surviving the first years and to building a thriving practice over time.

Before we dig into the details of how to survive and then thrive in practice, I want to offer some encouragement by dispelling a common myth about A/OM practice, detail why private practice offers those entering this profession the best option for earning a living, and then share some of my experiences in the hope it will help you realize that if I could build a successful practice, you can too.

Myth Busting

There is a rich tradition in many of the Asian arts regarding the respect afforded teachers or Masters. I have great respect for this tradition and consider myself to be extremely fortunate to have studied with some truly remarkable Masters. I am talking about those with seemingly mystical abilities that were trained in the ancient disciplines from childhood. One thing I learned from being around those of the highest skill level is that nobody cures everybody. I don't care who the Master is or how remarkable a healer they are, everyone has their failures. No one is successful even 90% of the time. I would estimate that the very best of the best are successful no more than 85% of the time and even that may be a little high. That means they will fail to "heal" their patients somewhere on the order of one out of every five times at best. Healing is (or at least should be) a very humbling art. You will have failures, even the very best do. I will be teaching you how to improve your odds of success and even how you can often turn your failures into a positive for your patients but you need to better understand the limits of any healing approach so you won't be too hard on yourself when those inevitable failures happen.

To help put the success/failure rate into perspective, consider what has been coming to light lately in some of the controlled clinical trials conducted on acupuncture. In many of these trials, researchers will test the effectiveness of points that have traditionally been recognized as being effective for the condition being studied against other points that are not even on known meridians. These are the so-called placebo or sham points. In many of these studies, the sham or placebo points are found to be surprisingly effective. In other words, acupuncture often gets good results in 40-50% of patients no matter where you put the needles! Many acupuncturists don't want to believe this but it is true. My theory about this is that sticking acupuncture needles in people causes the body to produce some anti-trauma chemistry or similar defensive reactions because the body thinks it has suffered some significant injury. This anti-trauma response can help many symptoms by itself especially pain-related ones. A recent study strongly suggests that this is the case.

If sticking needles anywhere can help 40%- 50% of some conditions and the very best Masters have about 80%-85% success rates, what success rates should we expect from a competent, journeyman acupuncturist? I would say somewhere in the 75% range. That is not such a great difference, is it? It is certainly not the primary factor that separates successful practices from those that fail. So don't worry. If you start out doing a good job on around 65% of your patients while you are learning how to improve your skills, you are still doing a respectable job for most of your patients—better than a lot of medical doctors do on the stubborn cases that often seek-out acupuncture. Too many acupuncturists get an inferiority complex because they think some of their teachers walk on water. They don't. And the myth of "mastery" gets inflated as people talk about how they cured someone with this or that condition while leaving out the fact that they also had some patients with the same condition they were not successful with.

Here is something one needs to keep in mind regarding acupuncture: It helps the body to better heal itself. I will be going into quite a bit of detail about that fact throughout this book but I mention it here to highlight the potential cure rates that happen when you help the body to heal itself. When you treat hundreds and then thousands of patients with this method of helping the body to heal itself, every once and a while, you will run across a case that responds in a really remarkable way—a miraculous cure. These rare cases happen because some people can develop serious conditions that actually need just a little push to help the body's resources gain the upper hand and heal the problem. Just like the saying about the straw that breaks the camel's back—sometimes lifting just a straw heals the camel's back. So all acupuncturists who see a high enough number of cases will have a few remarkable ones in which the treatment seems like magic.

Some acupuncturists will then point to these cases as though they get such miracle cures routinely. Baloney. No one routinely has miracle-type success. I can tell you about my patient with 40 years of back pain that was cured with one treatment and never had that problem again or the patient with M.S. who was deteriorating rapidly and had such a turn-around with treatment that her doctors later thought she never actually has M.S., but these cases are not the norm. They are just the much better-than-normal responses based on the law of averages that are bound to happen if you see enough cases. There will always be some cases that do better than average and some that do worse than average. Some acupuncturists brag about the ones that do better than average while neglecting to mention their failures and this makes many starting out in this profession feel like they will never match-up. You will match-up if you can learn how to establish the value of your services for your market and survive your first years in practice while getting the experience needed to reach journeyman competency at the two primary skills of marketing and patient satisfaction.

If you can survive your first years in practice and see enough patients to refine your skills to the point that you are helping three out of four of your patients, you will be doing far better than most other health care providers and laying the foundation for a very successful and secure practice. Getting through school and getting licensed should allow you to have the knowledge-base needed to succeed once you add the practical information of just what it takes to survive in private practice that is largely missing from the current A/OM training. It will take hard work and dedication, but nothing less should be expected in achieving the blessing of earning a comfortable living while helping others.

CHAPTER TWO

Making the Case for Private Practice

While the bulk of this book is about helping you to succeed in practice, I think it will be useful to start by considering why private practice offers the best chance to make a living for most entering this profession. I want to explore this because many of you may have your doubts about opening your own practice and be tempted to take a position that really does not work for you just because you are afraid to strike-out on your own. I occasionally give talks at acupuncture colleges and when doing so, I like to ask students what they plan to do once they graduate and pass the licensing exams. Virtually everyone I have asked this question to answers that they hope to start out by first working with an established practice, such as some sort of multi-disciplinary center or with another acupuncturist, chiropractor, or medical doctor. I don't recall a single student telling me they expect to go right out and begin their own practice.

I understand that for most, the idea of jumping into a solo private practice as soon as one gets their license is a scary thought. It would seem to be a safer transition to get started by working with others who are already out there practicing themselves whether as an acupuncturist or some other medical modality. I agree this would be an ideal way to start to learn the ropes, unfortunately such opportunities are few and far between as reflected the NCCAOM's JTA study showing only 12 % of Licensed Acupuncturists working in anything other than private practice. Don't you think most of those 88% in that survey working in solo private practice would like to be working in a multi-practitioner setting? Many undoubtedly tried for those types of jobs just out of school but could not find any or they possibly found some sort of position they thought would be good for them that didn't work out and eventually ended-up on their own.

The fact is that up to this point in time, it is a very rare situation in which an existing practice would want to bring-in an acupuncturist—especially one just out of school. Sure, you can find those willing to sub-lease you some office space in their practices (especially chiropractors) but most of those types of opportunities will be from someone who is struggling themselves and are just looking for help paying their rent. These practitioners are not the best ones to partner-up with and try to learn from. You need to be careful about just what you may get yourself into. Building a practice is not easy and for those practices that are doing things correctly, adding another practitioner who does not bring their own patient-base with them does not make financial sense in most instances. I will explain why this is so a little later.

There are two basic types of settings one might hope to land some sort of opportunity in an existing practice. One is coming into an existing acupuncture/Oriental Medicine practice and the other is getting into an integrated, multi-discipline practice. Let's look at both of these options and think logically about their viability:

Unlike what can be found in some physical therapy clinics, there are not many busy acupuncture clinics that have several acupuncturists working in them that would need to hire a new practitioner just out of school. I am not saying there is not a single one of these types of practices, just that they are very rare. This would be an ideal way for many to get started in this career and I hope such clinics become more plentiful over time, but there are not many now so if you should find such an opportunity, make sure you read all the fine print in any contract (or seek professional advice) and if it all checks-out, grab it and consider yourself one of the very lucky few. The vast majority of acupuncturists starting out, however, should not count on being so fortunate and need to face this reality.

What about a smaller practice then? Perhaps a solo practitioner who has gotten so busy that they need to bring in another acupuncturist to help them manage their overflow? While such a scenario is more likely than finding a position in a big, busy, multi-acupuncturist clinic, finding a solo practitioner ready to bring another acupuncturist into their practice is also rare. Why? First of all, the unfortunate fact is that there are not many acupuncturists who get to the point that they are so busy they are having trouble handling their patient load. This can be seen in NCCAOM's JTA stats showing only 9% grossing over $120k. That's why I wrote this book, remember? Secondly, if you find an acupuncturist fortunate enough to need to bring someone in, this is going to be a big deal for that acupuncturist. They are taking a chance bringing someone else into their good thing. They worked hard to get to the point they are having trouble handling their patient load and they could always just turn patients away when they can't accommodate any more. The minute a practitioner like that brings someone else in they are going to have to give-up some of their patients to help get the new practitioner off the ground. I will explain this further as understanding this can also help those with successful practices who may want to bring in another practitioner.

When a busy practitioner shifts some of their patient load to the new acupuncturist they just brought-in, they will experience a drop in income in the beginning. Of course, the hope is that eventually, the two together will build up the patient volume allowing the new practitioner to give a big enough percentage of their income to the original practitioner and eventually benefit both of them financially. It is also attractive to someone who has been working by themselves for some years while they built their practices to work with someone else as two heads are better than one. So while the hope of making more income and having a partner to work together with can be attractive to a busy solo practitioner, the logistics of pulling this off successfully are very difficult.

Successful solo acupuncture practices become successful because the acupuncturist was able to win the trust of their patients. People are skittish about having needles poked in them and tend to build strong loyalties toward their acupuncturist. It is not easy for an established practitioner to bring-in another acupuncturist and just turn over some of his or her patients to the new practitioner. The patients will not be very comfortable with being handed over to the new practitioner especially one recently licensed. Finding just the right person to bring into an established practice becomes essential. It is almost like choosing a spouse; it has to seem like the best fit possible on many levels. It is not easy to find someone like that. I would know. I've tried to find such a partner without success (I mean acupuncturist partner, I found the right spouse on my second try).

Another problem with bringing in a second practitioner is that this may require moving into a bigger office. If the established practitioner was smart, they would have kept their overhead low by leasing space that was not bigger than they needed for themselves. If they are now going to bring in a second practitioner, this could require a move to a bigger office with a higher overhead and the considerable hassle moving a practice entails. The same thing goes for front office staff. However the established practitioner has been managing their insurance billing, recordkeeping, and other front office responsibilities, doubling the number of practitioners by adding a second will require a significant change in how the office is run. These obstacles can be overcome of course, but the bottom line here is that with so few acupuncturists finding themselves busier than they can mange by themselves and the numerous problems associated with adding a second practitioner, few such positions await those trying to establish themselves in this profession.

The possible exception to the absence of a job market for acupuncturists is the occasional opportunities in Community Acupuncture clinics. As I will explain in more detail in the chapter on practice models, Community Acupuncture clinics operate under a high volume, low fee system and are growing rapidly. While the high volume of patients these clinics strive for has the potential to create demand for employees, those positions still tend to be quite limited and demand skills not many new graduates have. The specialized skills such clinics require mean that most Community Acupuncture clinics are hesitant to hire those just out of school.

Multi-Disciplinary Centers

How about finding a position in a multi-disciplinary practice in which you might be the only acupuncturist working with other disciplines such as Chiropractors, Physical Therapists, Massage Therapist, and Medical Doctors?

While the idea of practicing "Integrative Medicine" in a multi-disciplinary center that brings several disciplines together is touted as a desirable goal, the reality is that most of these centers struggle to make things work. The reason for this is that many of the so-called "Alternative" or "Complementary" therapies share a great deal of overlap in their patient base. Do you know the number one reason people in the U.S. seek-out acupuncture? You should. The number one reason is for back pain. What do you think is the number one reason people seek-out chiropractic or massage or physical therapy? Again, it is back pain. While there are plenty of people out there with back pain to go around, it is financially unfeasible to treat a condition like back pain with multiple disciplines when each of these disciplines have evolved as a stand-alone therapy. Treating a patient with back pain with acupuncture and chiropractic and massage therapy is just not cost effective especially considering the limits in insurance coverage.

Because cost factors require keeping the number of therapies down, in a multi-disciplinary center, someone must decide which therapies will be used for what patients and this tends to cause some resentment and competition between disciplines. So while the idea of blending many different types of therapies sounds great, in the real world these types of centers are not blossoming. Many open with high expectations and then struggle. Some end up with each discipline fending for themselves, carving-out their own patients and only rarely cross-referring to other disciplines. I worked in such a center for a short time in which I was lead to believe they needed an acupuncturist because their patients were asking for it after the previous acupuncturist had left. I came to find out the previous acupuncturist had worked hard to build his clientele but got so frustrated with the manner in which the center operated he left understandably taking most of his patients with him. After seeing few patients referred to me from the other disciplines, I also left and the center soon closed.

The lesson here is that there are very few centers that have multiple disciplines working in an integrated fashion that will need an acupuncturist because they have patients they want to refer for that service. In most of these centers, the individual disciplines will have to fend for themselves in building their own patient base. While there may be some advantages to trying to build a patient base within such a facility rather than your own private practice, there are also several downsides. You may be limited in how you market your services, or even the hours you can work, how you bill, etc. The bottom-line in such a setting is that you have less control over your own destiny as the center may go belly-up leaving you stranded or they might just decide they don't want to offer acupuncture anymore.

As in my warnings about finding a position in an acupuncture practice, I am not saying it is impossible to land a position in a multi-disciplinary center that works for all parties involved, just that it is very rare. Although opening your private practice certainly has risks, depending on others for your livelihood carries a lot of risks too. I wanted to stress the harsh realities of the very limited opportunities of finding a position in an established practice because those entering this field need to face the fact that private practice is the only viable means of making a career out of A/OM for the vast majority who become licensed in this field. It is far better for you to come to terms with this and *plan* for it so you have the best chance of making a success of it.

The very significant upside to opening your own private practice is that you have much more control over your own destiny. And, depending on your financial needs, it does not have to be so stressful. As you will read, in my case I began my practice under very stressful circumstances of trying to quickly become the sole source of income for my family of four. While I hope most of you aren't under as much financial stress, it is possible to make it work even under those circumstances as my example shows.

You know, it's kind of funny. When I started my practice in 1986 almost no one getting out of school at that time had any thoughts of doing anything other than going right into private practice. There were not any "integrative" or "CAM" medical centers and acupuncture was still viewed with extreme skepticism by most doctors so there was little thought of working within someone else's practice. 10-15 years later, when I spoke at acupuncture schools and all those students told me they were hoping to get positions in other practices, I was a little jealous that none of those opportunities were available to me when I first graduated. Now that I have been paying more attention to what is happening in the A/OM job market, hearing horror stories, and seeing the most recent stats, I realize that having no chance of anything but private practice was actually a very good thing for me. This kept me from any illusions of avoiding the risks of private practice when starting out. I now see that there are many advantages to starting an A/OM career in private practice and this perspective together with the right advice on how to make it work is badly needed by those entering this profession.

Building a practice does not have to be so scary. Your skills are badly needed and you can operate with very low overhead so setting up a private practice does not require much of an initial investment beyond your schooling. When you consider the vast array of conditions acupuncture can treat and that only something like 3% of Americans have ever had acupuncture, the potential for growth of the patient base for A/OM is tremendous. So while it is true that there are risks to building a private practice that must be approached carefully, it is also true that making your living in an A/OM practice is achievable while also being a truly wonderful blessing. If you achieve this blessing, you will be one of the most fortunate of all people including other healthcare professionals. You will be helping all kinds of people with all kinds of problems and doing so in a very safe way. You won't get wealthy but if you factor in the gratitude of your patients as part of your reward, you will enjoy a richness in your vocation few enjoy today.

A successful A/OM private practice office can be like a little oasis of calm, positive, healing qi in a stressed-out world. People will tell you how wonderful it is to come into your office, how peaceful and positive it feels. This is so different from many medical practices where they dole out drugs that cause side-effects and often fail to effectively address the cause of people's problems. Many of those offices have stressful qi about them because doctors are trying to treat 8-10 patients an hour and can never afford to spend the time necessary to connect with their patients. The Western medical profession as a whole is under increasing pressure as patient satisfaction is dropping and stresses within the doctor/patient relationship are rising. Your practice can be like an antidote to the souring that is taking place within the healthcare system in our society.

Just keep in mind that that you are not "settling" for a private practice because there were no jobs out there. A private A/OM practice is an honorable and more than 2,000 year-old tradition. While times change and many changes have and are taking place in A/OM, the practice of individuals helping the suffering of other individuals is as old as humanity and will always be so. To be able to make a career out of your humble practice helping those who are not being helped in the impersonal, high-tech system of modern medicine is a blessing deserving serious effort.

For now and for the foreseeable future, the best chance those entering this profession have to make a living in this field is to make it in private practice and this is where we should be focusing our efforts to improve training. I hope salaried jobs in hospitals or large centers will one day materialize but common sense should tell us that even if they do, they will always be only a small part of the overall job balance for A/OM practitioners. If good paying hospital and multi-disciplinary clinic jobs start to become plentiful, the acupuncture schools will crank up their student recruiting efforts and there will be a huge increase in the numbers of those entering this profession creating many more applicants vying for these positions. I will comment more about the dynamics within the A/OM profession's organizational structure toward the end of this book but just want to again stress that learning the realities of successful private practice should be seen as a fundamental part of your A/OM education.

CHAPTER THREE

My Story

My first exposure to acupuncture took place in 1965 when I was 10 years old. My sixth-grade teacher had recently returned from spending some years in Japan as a missionary and he showed our class several pictures of Japanese sights. One picture was of an Asian gentleman with a couple dozen acupuncture needles sticking into his face. Of course, this picture was fascinating to us kids and during the next recess, my best friend and I took some straight pins from a corkboard and tried to acupuncture ourselves. It hurt like heck and my friend and I quickly decided acupuncture was the dumbest thing we ever heard of and as for myself, I never gave acupuncture another thought until nearly a dozen years later.

When I was 17, I injured my back while working at a plastics factory when about 2,000 five-gallon plastic plant containers slammed a piece of wood into my spine causing a hairline fracture of my L5-S1 vertebra. I was off work for 7 weeks but the physical therapy did little good and my low back pain continued to bother me. Two years later, I went to my local library to find a book on back exercises and ran across a book on the Japanese system of Shiatsu acupressure. I had been a wrestler in high school and also developed an interest in martial arts and it was my respect for the Asian martial arts that prompted me to check-out the book on Shiatsu. By the way, many Americans of my generation who became involved in A/OM did so after involvement in the martial arts mainly thanks to the work of Bruce Lee. I found this book interesting and the author seemed knowledgeable but it was more of a book on how to perform Shiatsu on others than how to help your own health problems.

A few years after reading that book, I learned of a place that taught acupressure in Santa Monica, California, and they were to have a Shiatsu master teach a 20 hour class. The teacher was Wataru Ohashi, a world-class body worker who just blew me away with his skill. While leaving that class, I picked up a flyer that had listings for different health related businesses and saw a listing that stated "Taoist Master Hua-Ching Ni; Acupuncture, Diet and Herb Therapy for the Treatment of Disease". At this time, I was living with a woman and we had a child together who was born with a serious intestinal disorder known as Hirschsprung's Disease that rendered all of his large intestine and part of his small intestine non-functional. Our son required several surgeries and was left with an ileostomy. The stress of caring for an infant with an ileostomy and other factors caused his mother to develop a strong case of hyperthyroidism and she was to undergo radiation therapy to destroy half of her thyroid gland. After learning from Ohashi that this other world of Oriental medicine existed, we decided to consult with Master Ni to see if acupuncture and herbs could help.

Master Ni had recently come to the U.S. to teach Taoism as well as practice Chinese medicine. He told us he was confident the hyperthyroidism would improve, and after 6 weeks of acupuncture, herbs and a strict diet, another thyroid scan was done showing no sign of disease. At this time I had no thought of becoming an acupuncturist but began to study Taoist philosophy, spirituality and history with Master Ni. I became more and more interested in studying Taoism, taking classes and reading the books Master Ni had begun publishing, but while I did practice acupressure/massage on myself, family and friends, I continued to work in construction to support my family.

My life changed dramatically when my first wife (we had married by this time) suddenly left. She had been harboring some deep emotional problems of which I was unaware (which is a nice way of saying I was a naïve fool who fell for the wrong woman). Our son had undergone his fifth surgery to connect what was left of his small intestine to his rectum. While this made it so he would no longer require an ostomy bag, it caused a new set of complications that I felt only I could manage. Few children in the world had survived with his reduced length of bowel so there was no model of caring for this sort of thing. Feeling that only I could provide the care he needed to survive, I quit work and we lived on my son's meager Social Security Disability income.

During this time, my study of Taoism greatly deepened including the theories of qi, yin/yang, and Five Phases. I learned that these concepts were the foundation of Taoist science first and only secondarily applied to Chinese medicine theory. Eventually, I was reunited with a former girlfriend, Gayle, we made plans to marry, and, as my son was now well enough to enroll in preschool, I was ready to get back to work. I didn't want to return to construction. The time I spent in the hospital with my son watching the remarkably dedicated and skilled doctors and nurses impressed me greatly. I also had seen remarkable things possible with Chinese medicine and after studying Taoist philosophy and science for some years now, I had an understanding of the basic principles behind Chinese medicine. I began looking at going to acupuncture school and then read an article in my local newspaper about an acupuncture school that had just opened in a neighboring town. I drove to the school to check it out that afternoon and found myself sitting in class the next day. I was now on the path to become an acupuncturist.

During my schooling Gayle and I married and a year later we had a child on the way. In California at that time, you had to pass two state administered examinations to become licensed (certified), the first was a written exam and the second called a "practical" exam. Everyone I talked to who had taken these exams said the written was the hard part and that if you passed the written the practical was easy. I passed the written exam on my first try, took the practical exam and found it was easy, then began looking for office space with a friend of mine who had also just become licensed. We decided to go into practice together as this would allow us to split expenses and support each other in growing the practice. I found a good office space for a reasonable price and the owner agreed to wait the few months until my license became official before we moved in. I signed a year lease that was to begin on January 1, 1986.

My wife and I borrowed some money from her parents that enabled us to buy a new mobile home in a family park near the city my new office was to be located and at the end of October 1985, my second son Bryce was born with some jaundice but otherwise in great health. I was looking forward to this new phase in my life; a new wife, a second child, a new home, and a new career. Then came a bombshell: I received notice from the state informing me I had not passed the practical exam and would have to wait several months before I could re-take it. I was in shock. I was sure I had passed with flying colors. I had even failed the point location part of the exam when I was sure I had scored 100% on that part. I appealed the results but this was denied and I had to figure out what to do.

Then, another bombshell: My friend with whom I was to go into practice told me she was pulling-out. Her husband decided it was too big of a financial risk and she was going to just try to practice out of her home. I didn't want to go back to construction until I could retake the practical exam and I had signed a lease. I decided to ask my friend to work out of my office until I passed the exam and I would pay all expenses. I needed her to be at the office so that I had someone licensed and legal to do acupuncture until I got my license. During that time I would concentrate on doing acupressure/massage techniques.

We opened the office in early January, 1986 in San Dimas, California; a very conservative community on the eastern border of Los Angeles County perhaps best known for its annual Western Fair. The space was a 400 square foot, ground floor corner office with two rooms joined by a small walk-through space and a restroom. To say I was on a very limited budget would be an understatement. Rent was $360 a month and while that was good I had almost no money for equipment. I could not afford to buy partitions to separate the treatment tables in the treatment room. I couldn't even afford treatment tables! I built my two treatment tables with four-by-four studs for legs, particle board for the bed bottom, then I bought three inch foam and some vinyl from an upholstery shop and sewed the coverings myself. My wife and I then came up with a system for dividing the treatment room with curtains strung-up on wires hung on with curtain hooks. We then found a sofa and loveseat for $150 to go into the front waiting room and I was given an old desk that I had to refinish to make presentable. The entire cost for my office furnishings was no more than $500.

It is tempting to say I then hung-out a shingle and was open for business but in fact, I could not afford the shingle. Someone I knew did a little sign making on the side so I traded some treatments for him to make my shingle which hung in a window no one could see from the street. Now I was open for business in my tiny office with no license to practice, a bartered sign no one could see, handmade treatment tables, a salvaged desk, and zero patients. Oh – and a wife and two children to support. My wife had went on maternity leave from her job and wanted to stay home to care for the baby and my first son who we now learned had also suffered some brain damage during his infancy and was developmentally disabled as well as having his physical disability (add one more bombshell to the list). She was really needed at home but there was no way to know if the practice would ever generate enough for us to live. Remember, this was 1986 and acupuncture was far less accepted back in those days especially in the conservative community I had settled in knowing not a single soul there. I forged ahead hoping I could make enough money to buy some time before my wife would have to go back to work.

How did I do? It was a real struggle but my wife got her wish to be a stay-at-home Mom. I was making rent by the end of the first month and all expenses at the end of the third month. I took the practical exam again, passed it and had my license by June of 1986 which was vital as my friend whose license we were operating under was not showing up much by this time. Those six months did afford me the chance to refine my acupressure/massage techniques especially the use of auricular points using pressure techniques and applying taped-on pressure spheres.

As challenging as those early months of practice were, I was on Cloud Nine. I was helping people with my own two hands in my own office and actually starting to pay the bills with the income I made helping others. When I quit work to care for my son, I had been working in construction and completed apprenticeships in two different trades. While it is true that it takes hard work to build a practice, it is a different type of hard work compared to something like working in construction. When you have struggled to support a family in that type of physically taxing work, you will never complain about the "hard work" of establishing an acupuncture practice.

While my young practice was thankfully operating in the black, the income was not covering all my family's living expenses and at the end of the first year we were flat broke. In addition to construction, I also used to do auto-body work and made extra money fixing-up cars and reselling them. To help pay for my acupuncture schooling, my wife sold the Camaro she had bought new four years before and to make-up for it, I had bought a wrecked 1965 Mustang and restored it. She loved that car but now we were forced to sell it too so that we could stay afloat. The $3,000 the Mustang brought-in gave us enough cushion to survive for the next 6 months and by before the end of the second year, the practice was making enough income to actually support my family of four albeit in a very modest manner.

In the years that followed, my income and patient-load steadily grew to eventually allow my family a comfortable, middle-class livelihood. By the end of my second year I was performing about 30 treatments a week (it is better to count the treatments per week rather than how many patients you see a week because you will often see a single patient more than once a week). By the fourth year this had grown to be around 50 a week. At this stage I could have kept growing but I made the decision to hold my patient load at around 50-60 treatments a week as I wanted to devote some of my time to helping spread A/OM to the public. I had begun working with a state acupuncture association and decided that our profession needed people who would offer some of their time to help A/OM grow to reach more people. My main interest was helping to spread the good word about this beautiful, safe medicine that can help so many conditions. However, I was very disappointed to learn the A/OM organizations were not really interested in doing this as they had other priorities.

During those 15 years when I held my patient load at 50-60 treatments per week, I tried to do what I could to help spread A/OM. I wrote a book explaining the early roots, practice, and concepts behind acupuncture and OM theory. I wrote that book because I felt our inability to explain how acupuncture began encourages skeptics to proclaim acupuncture was started for superstitious reasons and not on a rational basis. I believe acupuncture was born out of rational influences and wanted to address this so I offered theories on not only how acupuncture likely began but how the theories behind the practice were likely inspired. I like to think this book is helpful to A/OM students as well. I also worked with the insurance industry helping to pioneer acupuncture HMO plans and I continued to lobby the leadership of our A/OM organizations about doing public education. Then, a year or two after moving to my third office, my patient-load started to grow both from my becoming better known in my community (despite my attempts to keep a low profile) and because I stared to get more and more referrals through the HMO plans I was a part of. For several years I was doing between 75-100 treatments per week out of my 750 square foot office mostly working out of two treatment rooms (with a third back-up room I rarely used). I recently moved into a 1400 square foot office with five treatment rooms and may eventually look to bring-in a partner to help me handle the demand.

Before you start doing the math and thinking I must be rich, you need to know I don't charge as much as many acupuncturists do so while I am happy with my income, I am not one of the bigger earners in our field and never had the ambition to be. I still like being able to have the time to undertake projects like writing this book. Having modest fees means I have to treat more patients to earn the same money I would with higher fees, but I like helping people and the more people you help, the more secure it makes your practice over time. I will be offering my advice about this dynamic and about establishing fees later.

While I have been very happy with the way my practice has worked-out to this point, my success has been bittersweet. One of the most influential teachings that inspired my respect of Taoism was a teaching credited to Lao Tzu that was destroyed centuries ago in China because there was controversy over whether or not it was a Taoist teaching or of Buddhist origin. This teaching is called the "*Hu Hua-Ching*", or "*The Classic of Refining the Undeveloped*". The first third of this classic is very similar to the Buddhist "*Diamond Sutra*". In the later part of the *Hua Hu-Ching* Lao Tzu is imploring other Taoists to stop being hermits and share their knowledge with the people. He said:

"It is the responsibility of one who can see to tell a blind horseman, upon a blind horse, that he is riding into an abyss."

We in the A/OM field can see that our gentle medical system is badly needed to supplement modern medicine's often overly-invasive methods. Most of the public is blind to this knowledge and we in the A/OM profession have a responsibility to help them see this. Because I made the decision to devote part of my career to helping people see this, I suspect I will continue to have mixed feelings about my "success" until the public's understanding of this healing system becomes much more widespread. I hope some of you reading this may join me in this effort as doing so will also help your chances of building a successful practice. I will offer more thoughts on this in my closing chapter.

CHAPTER FOUR

Practice Models – Emperor's Medicine, Peasant Medicine, and the Middle Way

I stated in the first chapter that while acupuncture has seen tremendous growth in its popularity over the last fifty years, little attention has been paid to just how acupuncturists can make a living offering that service. The subject of how to deliver acupuncture in a practical and sustainable manner that allows acupuncturist to earn a living is the subject of practice models. As I pointed-out in Chapter Two, about the only model most A/OM practitioners have available to them today in the West is private practice. Within the private practice model, there are a variety of models possible also. Before you can build a successful practice, you must decide just what type of private practice model you will pursue. There are many factors to consider but as far as income generation goes, the most important is deciding the volume or patient load you hope to build and the rate you will be charging for your services. As a general rule, most practices with a higher volume of patients will have relatively lower fees while those with lower volumes will have higher fees. The range between these two ratios can be remarkably wide in different practice models.

I once heard of an acupuncturist who practiced a type of Korean Constitutional acupuncture—a system using a spring loaded needle taking just few minutes to complete a treatment—who charged $10 a treatment and saw around 100 patients a day. Then there are some acupuncturists who take 1 ½ to 2 hours with every patient and charge $200 or more per treatment. Other than these rather extreme examples, the more typical higher volume/lower fee models charge fees of around $30 per treatment seeing 3-4 patients an hour. In my state of California with its large Asian population, you tend to see this model being practiced more by Asian practitioners perhaps catering mainly to Asian patients although that is just a general trend and there are many exceptions. At the lower volume/higher fee end of the spectrum, fees of around $80-$150 per treatment and seeing 1-2 patients an hour are fairly average.

Unfortunately, we don't have any statistics regarding how many practitioners are charging at what rates and how many patients on average they are seeing so we can't really compare different models to say which is working best on average. The stats of the 2008 NCCAOM's Job Training Analysis showing only 8.8% grossing over $120,000 per year suggests that neither model is doing particularly well. It may be that the fee charged per treatment is not a crucial factor for successful practice but until we have strong evidence proving this, I think it safest to assume fees play a major role in practice building.

The model that I developed and want to promote here is a **low overhead, moderate patient volume** (8-12 per day), **with a low rate of patients' average out-of- pocket expense**. What I mean by a low rate of my patients' average out-of-pocket expense is that I charge rates that are a little higher than most high volume/low fee practices but considerably less than the low volume/high fee practices and I accept insurance. I say "average" out-of-pocket expense because I charge different rates for children, adults, and seniors and then some of my patients who have insurance coverage will often just be making a co-payment. I will go into more detail about my fee structure and setting fees in the next chapter and the subject of accepting insurance later. The main point I wish to stress here is that in order to have the best chance to survive your first years in practice, you should pursue a model that strives to keep your patients' out of pocket costs low while not requiring you to see a high volume of patients in the beginning to survive. I call this model the *Middle Way* because it is somewhere between the high volume/low fee and low volume/high fee ones and also because that term has great significance in Taoist philosophy.

There is no single practice model that works best for everyone in every circumstance. Ultimately, the value of your services is what your local market is willing to pay. Just what people are willing (or able) to pay varies greatly due to many factors. The saying "Where there is a will there is a way" can apply to practice models. If you have a strong desire to make a certain model work you should go for it but be prepared to take a few years to get it there. I believe the Middle Way model I propose is the type that will work best for most to establish themselves as it essentially splits the difference between the stress of trying to build a practice while charging high fees and one requiring a high volume of patients. This model affords practitioners time to improve their clinical and marketing effectiveness and pay the bills while growing one's patient volume. Again, your biggest challenge is those first few years, once you get established you will be under less stress as you steadily build from your sound foundation.

Opening a practice once licensed is like a 16 year old who has just gotten his or her drivers license. You went through a phase where you learned the rules and theory, then a phase where those with experience looked over your shoulder while you took the wheel yourself. Now you are on your own but it will take a few years of experience before you are a qualified, journeyman driver. During your first years in practice, you should get experience in a wide range of skills necessary to market and manage a practice like insurance billing, communicating with your patients, and getting better and faster at your treatments. Once you gain that experience, you can then decide if you want to modify your practice to a higher fee or higher volume one.

While there is no single model that works for all, there are some basics that successful practices will tend to have in common. To illustrate this, I will use the example of two other practice models that are radically different on one hand and yet actually have some important areas of agreement on the other.

Emperor's Medicine

At one end of the practice model spectrum is a rather unusual model taught by Robert Doane, a dynamic individual with a forceful personality who exudes confidence. This model is one that charges fairly high fees but, under Mr. Doane's direction, he manages to service a high volume patient load. That is a different ratio than other higher-cost per treatment practice models that consider 30-40 treatments per week to be their target volume. Being that this model charges a fairly high rate, one practicing this would not necessarily need to have a high patient volume to survive.

Mr. Doane encourages practicing what he calls "Emperor's Medicine", meaning a comprehensive suite of services to help virtually every medical problem a patient may have somewhat like the level of care a Chinese Court physician treating the Emperor would have been responsible for in China's past. Mr. Doane apparently made his fortune in business and was introduced to Chinese medicine after he had retired, becoming so interested he went to school and became licensed. He then studied with some highly experienced teachers and opened a practice on an island in Washington State. After studying with a practice building organization well-known in the Chiropractic field, he modified that model to fit an A/OM practice.

An important component of Mr. Doane's model is encouraging patients to buy a block of treatments in advance at a discount over his regular rates. To his credit, he states that he and his associates will give a prorated refund if it turns-out the patient did not need as many treatments as was first estimated and will give additional treatments at no extra charge if they turn-out to need more. This model stresses that getting patients to pay in advance for the treatments they need has many advantages. This helps make the patient more committed and invested in the successful outcome of their treatment, takes the stress off both patient and practitioner regarding paying for treatment on an ongoing basis, helps put the practitioner on firmer financial ground, and takes fuller advantage of the placebo effect in healing.

While many may balk at the idea of getting patients to shell-out a few thousand dollars in advance, many chiropractors have done this for some time and Mr. Doane as an astute businessman has refined this approach within his practice model. He also has a program where he takes-on a limited number of acupuncturists to work in his office to be trained in his system as he states he wants to help others learn his methods and intensive training is the best way to do this. He also teaches CEU courses sponsored by Lotus Herbs. I took a one-day training from him and this is where I learned what I explained above. At that seminar, Mr. Doane stated he charges $120 a treatment but then gives a discount to $80 when a patient pays for the block of treatments. His office offers a free consultation and explains their process to each prospective patient at that time and usually will encourage patients to have four treatments in order to better determine how many more treatments will be needed and that is when the block of treatments will be offered. There are many more details to Mr. Doane's model and I encourage anyone interested in learning more to contact Lotus Herbs for seminar information or Mr. Doane's office.

While this model has been successful for Mr. Doane and (from what I hear) some of his students, one concern I had was over the legal considerations of charging in advance for future care. I have not tried to research this as I have no intention of using this model myself but would caution anyone considering doing so to learn the legal ramifications that will vary from state to state. This is the sort of information your state A/OM association should be able to help you with. The other concern I have with this model is the weight of responsibility that is taken on, especially for someone just out of school. I am not sure how many newer to practice are ready to be an Emperor's physician.

Peasant Medicine

At the other end of the practice model spectrum are the folks associated with the Community Acupuncture Network who practice what they call "Community Acupuncture." This practice model was pioneered by Lisa Rohleder who founded the Working Class Acupuncture clinic in Portland, Oregon in 2002 and help found the Community Acupuncture Network in 2006. Ms. Rohleder often refers to acupuncture as "Peasant Medicine", as it has been used in the Far East by the common masses often at very low cost. The Community Acupuncture clinics operate under a model that is high volume, low treatment charge on a sliding scale of between $15–$40 a treatment with the patient deciding how much they wish to pay without any sort of income verification or other qualifying. While the forgoing sentence describes the basic practice model for a Community Acupuncture clinic, it does not describe the soul of their model which is connecting to one's local community in a productive, integral, and humble way. It is also about providing a strong support network for other acupuncturists to make a reasonable living practicing Community Acupuncture.

Just as many might second guess the viability of charging patients thousands of dollars up-front as in Robert Doane's Emperor's Medicine model, many would also second-guess the viability of a model that charges on an elective sliding scale of $15-$40 a treatment. But, like the Emperor's Medicine model, the Community Acupuncture's Peasant Medicine model has been refined over several years and was carefully put together after Ms. Rohleder had worked in other types of Low-Cost clinics that relied on different types of funding grants to stay in operation. She came to believe reliance on outside funding was a significant obstacle to providing lower cost treatments in a sustainable manner. She and her associates crafted and refined their Working Class Acupuncture clinic model and built it into a sustainable clinic serving hundreds of patients a week. She considers the work she and her associates are doing to be nothing short of a revolution in the manner in which acupuncture is delivered and she pulls no punches in her criticisms of what she refers to as the "acu-establishment" – the collection of schools, organizations, and leaders in the established acupuncture field. Ms. Rohleder has been a lightening rod in the A/OM profession garnering both passionate support and admiration from some and contempt from others.

Despite this controversy, there can be no denying that this Community Acupuncture's Peasant Medicine model is having a significant impact on the manner in which acupuncture is being practiced. Since its inception, the Community Acupuncture (C.A.) model has been followed by over 150 clinics in the U.S. and several are being opened in other countries, making this the fastest growing model in the nation and perhaps the world. Most C.A. clinics treat their patients in a large room rather than in individual treatment rooms and utilize recliners rather than treatment tables. C.A. acupuncturists—or acu-punks—as they often refer to themselves, will then treat 6-7 patients at a time as these patients recline in their recliners in a single room. Most C.A. acupuncturists employ acupuncture techniques that don't require patients to disrobe, especially techniques using points in the lower arms and legs. C.A. acupuncturists find this type of treatment approach to be quite successful and they have a very robust support system to help those who decide to participate in the C.A. movement. In fact, I would say it is the great effort the CAN people put into developing their support system that has helped fuel the rapid growth of this model.

Community acupuncturists stress that most patients who could benefit from acupuncture need frequent, regular treatments and that too many acupuncturists have been encouraged to charge rates that make it impossible for most Americans to afford the treatments they need. This being the case, patients get under-treated which causes their results to suffer and this ends up hurting the success and growth of both individual practices and the profession as a whole. By allowing patients to decide what they can afford within the C.A. sliding scale, patients can afford to get the treatments they need, success rates increase and practices grow as a result. The C.A. model does not advocate accepting insurance payment and the sliding fee structure might prohibit this although some individuals working within that basic system might have found a way to do so.

While these two practice models could not be farther apart in their fee structures, payment methods, and ultimate income expectations, they actually share some important things in common regarding how to improve success rates with patients. Both models are built around attempting to ensure patients get the number of treatments they need in order to be as successful as possible. Both also seek to lessen the stress of producing results deemed worth the costs to their patients albeit in a very different manner. In other words, both models address the stress of charging for a service when the outcome is uncertain. The Emperor's Medicine model does this by committing to doing as many treatments as it takes to help the patient at a fixed price while the Peasant Medicine model does that by making the treatment costs low enough that the patients can afford more treatment with less stress as compared to treatment with higher treatment fees.

Many practices charging higher rates paid for at the time of service constantly struggle to keep producing good enough results so that patients feel they are getting a good value. Too many practices that charge higher rates—say over $60 a treatment or so—try to get by treating their patients once a week because they are afraid the patient can't afford more. But, by starting off the treatment this way, they often don't get good results because they are under-treating. Patients will tend to come two or three times, see little or no improvement and then stop coming because they don't feel the treatment is worth the cost.

I wholeheartedly agree with both Robert Doane and the Community Acupuncture folks that one needs to pay great attention to being able to treat often enough to get the most out of acupuncture and to be sensitive as to how the issue of affordability will be perceived by the patient. If you under-treat, you will not get the most consistently good results and this will seriously hinder the ability of your practice to grow. Then again, if you over-treat, this will raise the costs of your services unnecessarily also hindering the growth of your practice. In socialized hospital settings such as was the case in China, they didn't worry much about over-treating because they didn't have the market pressures regarding costs that we have here. Since it is almost impossible to cause any real harm with acupuncture, the only risk associated with over-treating is the cost of the treatment or the time required of the patient. If there are no cost concerns, it is better to err on the side of over-treating to be sure you obtain the best possible benefit from the treatment. In the Middle Way model, you try to get the most benefit with the least out-of-pocket cost without over or under-treating. This is a delicate balancing act but it is the way to help make your services a good value for your patients. I will be offering lots of advice on how to pull-off this balancing act.

As you will learn, success in private practice comes from paying attention to details and not just skills like being great at diagnosis or having wonderful needling technique. Both in caring for the health of your patients and caring for the health of your practice, it really is a matter of "every little bit counts." In ancient China, they often used metaphors to describe treating health problems that evoked images of engaging in a battle. Doctors were battling the disease and had to approach their treatments with the same care as a General fighting a determined enemy. After many years in practice, I understand why those metaphors were used. Like a battle, you must pay attention to detail and not get lazy or complacent. You need to be prepared to fight for every bit of progress and be on guard for surprise attacks (unexpected complications). Once you gain ground, you need to work to hold it and then move forward again.

In the following chapters, I am going to put my model for practice building into perspective by breaking things down to their most basic elements. What I especially want you to become more aware of is just how a patient or prospective patient views you and the services you offer. The better you learn to see things from their point of view, the better you will be able to achieve a high rate of patient satisfaction. I will explain after I touch on the subject of establishing fees that patient satisfaction is the foundation of a successful practice.

CHAPTER FIVE

Establishing Your Fees

There are several major decisions you must make to give yourself the best chance to survive in private practice and near the top of this list is the question of how much you will charge for your services. I mentioned in the previous chapter that the model I promote focuses on maintaining a low overhead, a moderate patient volume, with a low average out-of-pocket cost to the patient. In this chapter, I want to delve into the issue of charging fees for acupuncture. As this is such a touchy topic with some people, I will go into detail explaining my perspective. Of course, this is my own opinion, others will have different opinions. What I will offer here is what I believe to be the most realistic price range for trying to build a practice in the broadest market segments.

The issue of how much acupuncture treatments are worth is relative; like many matters in the marketplace, a service like acupuncture treatment is ultimately worth what people are willing to pay, including third-party payors such as insurance companies. As I stressed in the beginning of this book, understanding the value of acupuncture services is not easy because it is difficult to know just how many treatments will be needed and different patients have different financial means and different ideas about what they believe to be manageable cost-wise.

Most acupuncturists make the mistake of setting their fees based on how much money they want or feel they need to make. Many have been taught that they should not "sell themselves short" by charging too little. Following this advice, they decide to charge $80-$120 per treatment, calculate how many patients they will need to see at those fees to make the money they want to make, and then try to build their practice to that patient load. What should be done is to realistically evaluate just what the market will bear—how to make the costs of your treatments a reasonable value for your patients. This will vary depending on your market, especially the area you are in. Are you going to open your practice in Beverly Hills, California or Jackson, Mississippi? We will consider issues related to practice location and patient demographics later; the main issue I want to cover here is the basic question of what is a reasonable charge for acupuncture.

If you look over the incredibly long history of acupuncture, you become overwhelmed at the various ways it has been utilized. It really has been employed in everything from Emperor's Medicine to Peasant Medicine and all points in between. In other words, you can't look back and find how it was "usually" done. The manner in which acupuncture has been delivered and paid for varies depending on the circumstances in which it is taking place. This means there is no "right way" acupuncture should be done to help you know how much you should charge to perform it this way. As I mentioned in Chapter One, in China officials have set treatment charges so low it is causing practitioners to leave that field. Just how acupuncture has been clinically performed over the years has been as much determined by the circumstances of the culture/market as the mechanics of how it works therapeutically.

In the West before any licensing laws were adopted, most acupuncture was done within the Chinese community in the private homes of practitioners or the back rooms of Chinatown herb shops. The fees for such treatment were often on the modest side although some acupuncturists might have commanded higher fees based on their reputations (deserved or not). When acupuncture burst on the scene in the early to mid 1970's after "New York Times" reporter James Reston wrote his article about his experience with acupuncture, the first regulation of acupuncture in the U.S. began. Many of the first practitioners licensed and now openly practicing under these new regulations set the tone for how acupuncturists ran their practices including how much they charged and how often they treated patients on average.

Being that acupuncture was so new to people in the West, many of the first non-Asian patients to seek-out acupuncture were those who were more "into" innovative—even "New Age" healing methods. These tended to be female, white, college educated, higher-income types and this demographic was the bread and butter clientele for the first generations of acupuncturists that were licensed in the U.S. Times have changed though and finding more and more of this relatively small patient demographic to serve as clientele for the rapidly growing acupuncture profession has not made sense for some years now. In my opinion, acupuncturists need to face the reality that seeing one patient an hour for one treatment per week and charging fees that would support a practice at this treatment pace and price points may have worked for some of the first generations of U.S. trained and licensed acupuncturists but cannot be counted on today to sustain our profession's growth. Some individuals are able to make this work, but not the profession as a whole.

I mentioned earlier that I work in the insurance industry. I was on the original panel of advisors that helped the insurance company American Specialty Health develop their first acupuncture HMO plan in 1997. The reason I was inclined to work with this company was my belief that the white, female, college educated, upper income clientele so many acupuncturists made their livings from was far too limited of a patient base to support our growing profession. Some of my colleagues on this advisory panel were leaders of acupuncture organizations and many of them were criticized for helping to create these HMO plans because the payment rates for acupuncture treatments were lower than what many acupuncturists charged. This was the first time that debates over how much acupuncture should cost were waged in public in the U.S. and it got pretty nasty. Those of us helping to build HMO plans with their modest reimbursement rates were made-out to be the Benedict Arnolds of the acupuncture profession. We fought as hard as we could to get reimbursement rates raised and won some modest concessions, but the fact is these rates really do reflect the state of the market. If enough acupuncturists are willing to work at these rates, then it is in the best interest of both the insurance companies *and* the patients to pay at those rates.

Critics could not accept this simple fact and claimed that these low rates would force acupuncturists to do a substandard job in their treatments. Acupuncturists, they said, could not afford to spend the time and take the care to do a good job for their patients at these rates and this would ultimately be harmful to the public. More recently, the Community Acupuncture supporters with their low fee sliding scale have also been heavily criticized with the same rationale. Let's examine this argument and see where it falls apart:

If the argument that lower rates for acupuncture means acupuncturists will have to see too many patients and will not be able to take the time to deliver proper care, then the acupuncture being done in the TCM wards of the hospitals in China must be the worst acupuncture in the world. In that setting, acupuncturists see dozens of patients a day and are paid very poorly for it yet I have never heard anyone publicly criticize that model or those acupuncturists working under those conditions. Where is the outrage over this? Some who charge higher fees feel justified in this because they believe themselves to be so much better than the average practitioner and maybe they are. However, if you look at the very studious and hard working colleagues of ours in those TCM hospitals as representing a pretty high level of practitioner, you can see that they often need many treatments to help their patients. Nobody routinely cures their patients with just a few treatments thus justifying charges that are truly worth 3,5, or even 10 times more than the lower fees some acupuncturists charge per treatment.

The ones who complain the loudest about those accepting low fees are the fortunate few who have been successful in carving-out a niche of clientele who can afford to pay substantially more or who have the unusual types of insurance clients whose policies pay high fees. I don't begrudge these people their good fortune. I think it is great they have been able to accomplish this because it is tough to make a living in this profession. These critics need to realize, however, that the vast majority of acupuncturists have not been able to make that model work for them and will not be able to do so moving forward. The bottom-line is if acupuncture can be done well at modest fees it is in the public's best interest to do so and focusing on the public's best interest is the wisest thing a health care profession can do.

If you charge higher rates, you greatly compound the stress to produce results that your patients feel are worth the costs unless you are servicing a rich clientele who expect to pay inflated prices. The higher your rates, the more valuable each treatment will need to be. If you charge $120 per treatment, will you be able to make your treatments at least three times more valuable than the acupuncturist across town who charges $40 per treatment? Are you ready to take on this extra pressure? A course of acupuncture treatment in China currently costs about sixty U.S. cents making it clear that there is no industry-wide guideline as to what "should" be the fee for acupuncture and much more thought needs to be given to this issue. What is being charged in China is surely too low and is causing problems in that system but their fee structure demonstrates just how great a range there can be in fees charged for acupuncture services.

Am I saying that charging lower fees is the key to practice survival? No. I am saying you have to be realistic about just what the market will bear, that the old model the first generations of U.S. trained and licensed acupuncturists employed to survive should not be followed uncritically, and that you should not be afraid of charging less if your market realities require this. I am also saying that if you charge on the upper end of your markets norm, you put yourself under greater stress to produce more results with fewer treatments. Think of it like going to a restaurant. If you go to a small Mom and Pop restaurant and they serve pretty good food at reasonable prices, you tend to be happy with the experience even if everything was not perfect. Go to a swank, high-priced restaurant and even if the food is great you might come away disappointed if the waiter didn't keep your water glass filled fast enough.

People are tired of being sold a bill of goods by slick marketers. If you come across as someone who is obviously not getting rich off your patients but are trying your very best to help them and the money is not your primary motivation, your patients will sense this and be very grateful. They will also be less demanding and more forgiving if you make some mistakes. They will be more willing to work with you as you try to help them. If you come across as someone who really cares deeply about helping them, it subtly shifts the responsibility for the outcome of the treatment from being all on your shoulders to a team effort in which the patient also bears some responsibility. This is how it should be. Patients should bear some of the responsibility for their therapy. It should not be 100% on your shoulders. If you give the impression that you are such a special healer and that is why your fees are high, the patient will expect you to be more responsible for their improvement and will not tend to work as hard themselves. I hope you give this some thought as building a constructive relationship with your patients will not only improve your patient satisfaction rates, it will reduce your possible liability, i.e.—the likelihood of being sued.

The Numbers

To the best of my knowledge, there has been no research comparing different types of acupuncture treatments to get an idea of what techniques get better results and thus have a greater value. One study that did look at the general issue of cost effectiveness was a study done in Germany on treating low back pain. This study was funded by German insurance companies and one of their conclusions was that acupuncture was cost effective for low back pain *if* the cost was under $50 P/T (per treatment). This figure caught my eye because it is in line with what I believe is a ball park figure for what the market will bear for acupuncture treatments in many private practice settings in the West. Most acupuncturists should be able to make a comfortable living charging in this range if they can build a moderate patient load.

The $50 P/T figure is just a rough one that can provide a realistic starting point that would need to be adjusted up or down depending on local market dynamics. Again, your services are worth what the market is willing to pay and I am only trying to offer my honest opinion as someone who has not only been in practice for 25 years but has been active in many aspects of the growth of the acupuncture profession including the insurance industry's coverage of acupuncture. No doubt some of the Community Acupuncture people will think this figure is too high, placing acupuncture out of reach for a large percentage of working class people, and those who have been getting two or three times as much for their treatments will think me foolish and even dangerous for advocating charging so low. No one practice model including a treatment fee guideline will work for everyone in every circumstance. But while this figure will be too high for some markets and too low for others, charging in this range will be affordable for tens of millions of middle-class people *if you can squeeze the most benefit out of the least number of treatments as I will be teaching you to do.* This price range should also work in all but the most expensive (high rent) areas and does not require seeing a high volume of patients to make a decent living.

If you calculate income based on a full-time practice being open five days a week, and averaging ten treatments a day, you end up with fifty treatments a week. If you average making $40 P/T and you averaged fifty treatments per week for fifty weeks a year, this would give you a gross income of $100,000 per year. With an overhead of 35%-40%, that would leave a before tax income of $60,000-$65,000 a year. That figure represents a healthy income that would allow most a nice living while being able to re-pay student loans. Tweak the figures of average treatments per week, multiplied by average fees, and subtracting overhead, and you can calculate a range of different pre-tax incomes. Lower your overhead, you don't have to gross quite as much to net in this range. If your market will allow slightly higher average fees, you won't have to average as many patients per week. If you can increase your patient volume by lowering your fees, this can help get you in the target range also.

Achieving a gross income somewhere in the $100k a year range should be feasible for most private A/OM practices if the practitioner is working full-time hours of forty to fifty hours a week. The greatest challenge you will face is surviving the first years while building-up to the patient volume you need to gross near the $100k range. It should not be unrealistic to hope to achieve this in two to three years. Some will be able to do this in less time. I will offer advice in Chapter Twenty on ways you can get off to the best start possible—to hit the ground running and improve your chances of earning enough to survive those crucial first years. Of course, no one can offer a strategy that will insure success for everyone. If you are coming out of school with $100k in student loans, only want to work part-time, and insist on opening your clinic in an expensive area already saturated with other established acupuncturists, you are almost certainly doomed to failure.

My treatment charges are currently $60 for adult patients, $40 for senior citizens (65 years of age and over) and anywhere from $10-$30 for infants to students depending on the time it takes to treat them. I mostly do qi-gong, acupressure and massage techniques on infants and young children and either those and/or acupuncture on older children. It is my understanding that many states do not allow charging discount rates for groups like seniors, my State of California being one of the exceptions. You should check into the legality of this in your state but I think it is easy to get around such dumb regulations by stressing your fees are based on time spent. I don't utilize quite as much time on my elderly patients and even less on my younger patients. If I was in a state that frowned on giving discounts to specific age groups, I would make sure I had some sort of written policy explaining this was due to the time factor. Many elderly patients especially need a price break as they are living on fixed incomes and Social Security does not pay for acupuncture.

With my current pricing structure, my patients' average out-of-pocket cost is about $24 P/T. Factoring in third-party reimbursement, the amount I average in total compensation for each treatment is about $43. Both of those figures can vary a bit up and down of course, but this means my total compensation on average is about 75% more than what the patient actually pays out-of-pocket. Yes, I do have some extra overhead involved with managing insurance billing, but it is nowhere near the 75% extra I receive as a result of accepting third-party payment.

The above figures do not include my herb sales. My policy on herbs is to only have a very modest average mark-up to cover the costs of the herbs and allow a small profit. I consider herbs to be part of my overall service and use them to help me achieve the goal of squeezing the most benefit out of the least cost to my patients. I always look for every advantage to improve the cost effectiveness of my treatments and herbs can be a big help in this. Some herbs are so expensive, I actually sell them at my cost while others are cheap enough to allow me to charge a bigger mark-up while still keeping them affordable. Just like I do with having a range of prices for my treatments that allows the higher profits ones to subsidize the lower profit ones, I have a range of mark-up for my herbs that allows me to keep the average price reasonable.

When I first opened my practice in 1986, I charged $40 for adults, $25 for seniors, and $10-$20 for children or students. I don't anticipate raising my rates in the near future except I might start to charge a modest additional fee for the first visit for adults and perhaps bump-up my rate for children a little. I know I won't be increasing my senior rates anytime soon. While I am in a position that I could raise my rates and do just fine if I were to lose some patients and have a little lower patient volume made-up for with a higher average fee per treatment, I would not feel right about putting my services out of reach for any of my patients. As I have thought back about this over my career, I realize that once my practice was well established, I could have easily raised my rates, weathered the fall-out, and shifted to catering to a higher income clientele. But when I think about all of the patients I was able to help who could not have afforded me if my rates were higher, I know I made the right choice. I feel honored that I was able to be of help to those patients. People with more money have more choices while people with less money need more choices. Our profession needs to have enough caring and qualified practitioners charging fees that provide a good value for all. That is why I have so much respect for the Community Acupuncture people even though I think that model may not be the best for some to establish their practices right out of school as it requires such a high patient volume to make it work financially.

I know some people look at the numbers and think it's better to work at establishing a practice with higher fees. You will only need to do half as many treatments charging $80 a treatment than if you charge $40 they will say. While this is true from a theoretical numbers perspective, there is another important reason to seriously consider developing your practice as one with modest fees and a somewhat higher patient volume. If you are doing your job right and achieving a high rate of patient satisfaction as I will detail in the next chapter, your chances of building a successful and secure practice will be much better the more patients you treat. Every satisfied patient you have is both a potential repeat patient and one who may refer others to you. Your ability to grow and sustain your practice over the years will depend on these satisfied patients and the more of them you create, the better your odds of future growth and sustainability. I mean, think about it: The more people you help, the better the chances you will achieve the blessing of earning a comfortable living.

I will give much more information on how to make my model work as far as the business aspects of practice building goes later in this book. For now, I want to get to the part I am most anxious to share with you—the fun part of how to provide this beautiful healing service to your patients in a way that works for both.

CHAPTER SIX

Patient Satisfaction

I sometimes teach a continuing education course I title *The Successful Management of the Low Back Pain Patient.* I like to start this topic by explaining just what I mean by "successful management" or more simply, what one should consider to be "success" with your patients. "Success" is not the same as "cure" and my advice to you is to forget the concept of "cure". The idea of curing medical conditions might be useful in research or public health arenas, but it is completely useless in private practice. We don't cure medical conditions, we manage patients. In the process of managing a patient, their medical condition may completely resolve and never return —what most would call a "cure"— but that should not be your goal. *Your goal should be to manage your patients in such a manner that you achieve the highest level of patient satisfaction.*

As I have stated before, operating a private practice is running a business. You are a self-employed small business person and your patients are similar to customers in any small business. Patient or customer satisfaction is the key to success in any service business. The definition of being "successful" with your patients then is when your patient is satisfied with your service. If your patient is glad they came to you after you provided your service, you were successful with that patient. Notice here I am not framing this in terms of how much you reduced your patients' symptoms or restored functioning, etc. The most important measure of success is the level of patient satisfaction and that is not always the same as success in reducing or eliminating their medical condition.

Believe it or not, it is possible that you could cure some patients of their condition and have them be unsatisfied with your service. On the other hand, it is also true that you might be unsuccessful in helping the medical problem your patient came to you for and still have him/her be very satisfied with your service. This being the case your patient satisfaction rate should be higher than the rate you are successful in providing substantial relief of the medical problem your patients came to you for. While, as I mentioned earlier, your success rate for relieving medical conditions should be in the 65%-75% range to start, you want to achieve a patient satisfaction rate of at least 90% and a dissatisfaction rate of no more than 2-3%.

While there is more to achieving the goal of a high rate of patient satisfaction than just clinical expertise in diagnosis and treatment, having those skills will of course make your job easier. High patient satisfaction rates happen when you can deliver a combination of three things: ***perceived benefit*** at a ***manageable cost*** via a ***pleasant experience***. If you can consistently provide a high percentage of your patients a perceived benefit at manageable costs and do so while creating a pleasant experience, you will have mastered the most important skills necessary to succeed in practice. Of course, as mentioned earlier, you must also learn how to get these patients in your door, but more on that later.

I will break these three factors down so I can explain them more thoroughly:

Perceived Benefit: I am using the phrase "perceived" benefit instead of saying "benefit" or "significant" benefit for an important reason. There can be a difference between actual benefit and your patient's perception of their benefit. While not too common, it is possible that a patient thinks (perceives) they are getting better when they are not. This rare occurrence would usually be to your benefit in managing your patients except in cases involving dangerous medical conditions like cancer. You need to guard against any patient with a serious condition who perceives they are improving when they are not especially if this causes them to forego other therapies they could benefit from like medications. What is far more common, however, is when patients think they are not getting any better when they actually are. This tendency to not perceive the subtle benefits of natural healing in the beginning stages of a treatment process is a big problem we will consider later in detail.

There are also cases when you are not successful in helping the problems your patients came to you for but you are still able to help them in other ways, especially helping other medical conditions or advising them on how to improve their overall health, etc. The goal is to see that virtually everyone who walks in your door seeking your help comes away with some perceived benefit.

Manageable Cost: I use the term "manageable" instead of something like "low" or even "affordable" costs because sometimes a patient may not consider your total treatment charges low or even affordable but if they can manage it, that is what counts. This is a bit of semantics here, but I like to choose my words carefully.

Pleasant Experience: Working on making sure your patients have a pleasant experience does not mean you have to pamper them overtly. Just put yourself in their shoes and try to make their contact with you and your office both personable and professional. This is the easiest of these three factors to control and I will cover this in more detail in the sections on managing the treatment process and your office.

The first two of these three factors—perceived benefit and manageable cost—together equate to the "value" of your services. If you can provide a good value and a pleasant experience, you will achieve a high rate of patient satisfaction. I will continue to break down the value of your service into the two categories of perceived benefit and manageable costs as this will allow for more detailed discussion of how to become competent in these skills. I just wanted to mention that these two equate to value because that is a term often used in resources on business skills that you might run across. As you will see, each of these three (and especially the first two) have a great deal of overlap so I will not be able to separate them completely and I will have to go back and forth a bit between issues such as how to space treatments and how to set treatment fees as these types of issues are interrelated.

Measuring Progress and Patient Satisfaction

One of the most important and subtle skills needed to obtain the highest patient satisfaction rates is the ability to measure even the slightest progress and help your patients perceive the benefits of the treatment. While many patients have no trouble noticing their improvement a surprising number won't. This is especially true in treating chronic conditions that your patient has had for a longer period of time and those types of patients are frequently seen in most practices. It took me some years to appreciate just how common it is for some patients to be unaware that they had made gradual progress. I think this happens for two reasons: First, acupuncture stimulates the body's own resources, boosting the body's efforts to heal itself and we usually are not aware of the effects of these resources. You don't "feel" a cut healing, for example. Second, I believe it is just human nature to focus on the problems that remain and not on what has improved, especially if that improvement was slight and gradual. Evolution has probably programmed us to focus on the problems that remain rather than wasting our limited resources on thinking how lovely it is that some old problem has eased. Whatever the reasons for this lack of awareness, it is something to which you had better pay close attention.

I couldn't count the number of times I have asked a patient how they have been since their last treatment, had them tell me they were "the same", and then had their spouse speak-up telling them they were crazy and that they had been doing things around the house they had not been able to do for months before starting treatment. The fact is we are not very objective observers of our own progress, especially if any problems remain. While you must of course give great weight to a patient's subjective assessment of their symptoms, be on guard against the tendency of underestimating progress.

You need to pay close attention and measure progress carefully so you don't lose a patient who thought they weren't improving when they actually were. There is a momentum to improvement that builds over time especially in treating chronic conditions. When you get even very modest progress, you want to strike while the iron is hot because there should soon follow a period where the pace of progress speeds-up. I tell my patients this is like growing a plant from a seed. Getting even modest improvement is like a sprout. It may not seem like much but if you keep nurturing the sprout it should hit a growth spurt. I will comment more on this phenomenon in the section on spacing treatments to spark and ride momentum in Chapter Twelve.

Another reason it is important to be able to measure any progress is you don't want to switch treatment plans thinking the first was not working when it was. Learning when to stay with your "Plan A" and when to switch to "Plan B" or "Plan C" is a very important skill that depends on your ability to accurately measure progress. In my first few years of practice, I tended to change treatment plans too quickly when the patients told me they were "the same" after two or three treatments and I feared I would lose them if I didn't make something happen right away. Once I got better at recognizing subtle improvements and started giving my original treatment approach a little longer, I saw many of these cases eventually show noticeable improvement with just a couple more treatments and my success rates went up. This is why it is so important to accurately detail the pattern of symptoms when you take your patient's history and monitor those symptoms during the treatment process. I will go over how to do this when I explain the intake process in the next chapter. I will also teach you my system for measuring progress in the section on measuring progress in the four (plus one) factors in Chapter Thirteen.

Being that most patients here in the West are unfamiliar with the way acupuncture works, many will "try" acupuncture but will only give it a limited number of treatments before stopping. I will go into this in more detail later; I mention it now because I just want to emphasize that you will usually have a limited window to establish a perceived benefit. Some practitioners try to address this by using techniques that can produce fast results in reducing symptoms, especially pain. There are several variations of such techniques including Richard Tan's "Balance Method." I have only taken one class and one short lecture from Dr. Tan and was surprised to find out much of what he taught (at the beginning-level class I attended) were techniques I had learned from one of my teachers during my schooling. I rarely use these techniques anymore but they are useful to have in your tool belt and I encourage you to get training in these types of methods. You need to gain your patients' confidence as early as you can for them to stay with the treatments long enough for you to help them the most and these types of methods can help.

You might wonder why I rarely use the techniques mentioned above that can cause a perception of benefit relatively quickly. I don't rely on these much anymore because, in my experience, the methods that cause quicker results also tend to wear-off more quickly. I generally focus on techniques that can be more subtle in the beginning but also are more stable on average in the long run. I am not saying my methods are better, especially as I did not try to learn the more rapid response methods to their higher levels. All acupuncturists need to eventually find their own methods that work best for them. No one method works best for everybody. At the higher levels of practice, acupuncture is an art and all artists need to find their own niche. Learning different techniques allows you a better chance of finding one or two that resonate with you—ones that seem to fit your own strengths. What I will be teaching you should help you achieve higher patient satisfaction rates whatever methods you practice.

CHAPTER SEVEN

The Intake

In this section, I want to explain my protocol for the critical intake process or what you should do once you have them in your door. For most of your patients, this will be the first time they have met you face to face, perhaps even the first time they have met an acupuncturist. You should approach the intake not only as a time when you get the information you need to evaluate the patient but also as the time your prospective patient will be evaluating you. To them, you are a stranger who wants to start poking needles in them for a fee and with no guarantee about the outcome. You have probably heard people say that word of mouth is the best way to build a practice. A big reason this can be true is that it eases the awkwardness of this first meeting. You can't rely on word of mouth alone, however, and even in those cases you still need to make a good first impression. This first meeting is where a prospective patient decides if they will become your patient and it also begins to establish your working relationship.

First off, I strongly encourage you to offer free, no obligation consultations. Most people don't understand anything about acupuncture so you should not charge a fee to explain to them what the treatment is all about. I offer a half-hour consultation, recommend they arrive a few minutes early to fill-out a brief intake form, and tell them that once I get the information I need I will let them know if I think I can help or not as well as answer any questions they may have. You want to use the intake process then, as the means by which you orient your patients to the basic treatment process and answer their questions. The most common questions a prospective patient will want addressed are:

1. Can your treatments (acupuncture) help my condition?
2. How many treatments will it take in total?
3. How many treatments will it take before I feel improvement?

Questions about the number of treatments are essentially questions about the cost of the treatment although even in those rare insurance cases where the patient might not have any out-of-pocket cost, they will still want to know how many treatments will be needed. These are all perfectly reasonable questions that you are not going to be able to answer with certainty. As a way of managing this potentially awkward situation, I have developed a protocol for addressing these questions and easing the understandable concerns patients have about the uncertain outcome. One of the keys to this protocol is being able to explain how acupuncture works in simple, straightforward language they understand. As you will see, the way I have learned to do this not only makes it easy for people to understand, it allows me to address the questions above and most any other questions my patients have both before and throughout the treatment process. This allows the two of us to be on the same page so we proceed not only with the patient being informed there is no guarantee about the outcome but understanding why this must be the case. Explaining things in this manner also makes the patient a better partner in managing their care and even increases the chances your patients will refer other prospective patients.

I address the first of these three questions by giving the prospective patient my honest estimate of whether or not I think the treatment will be successful for them. I literally give them an estimate of the odds the treatment will be successful as I will explain later. I don't do a full examination at this time because it is not needed to give that estimate. All that is needed at first is the history of the patient's pattern of symptoms (I will explain that later, too). I do the exam I feel is needed before actually starting their first treatment. Other than occasional cases of acute, minor injuries, most patients seeking acupuncture have chronic conditions requiring several treatments over several weeks and the information I will be giving you here addresses those types of patients.

The second question regarding the total number of treatments needed is the most difficult to address. While I will give an estimate of the number of treatments I believe it will take overall, I actually try to avoid this when possible. It is just a fact that it is impossible to know exactly how many treatments it will take to help your patients as much as you can—what in the insurance industry is called reaching "maximum therapeutic benefit." There are too many factors influencing this that you cannot control or predict accurately for everyone. You should, however, be able to get a much better idea of the number of treatments that will be needed in the end by monitoring how your patient progresses in the beginning of the treatment process. Once you have this better estimate, you let the patient know.

I try to shift my prospective patient's focus more to the third question of how many treatments it should take to see any improvement. To do this, I tell them that acupuncture is both therapeutic and diagnostic and that with each treatment I will learn a little more about how the treatment is proceeding and whether we seem to be meeting, exceeding, or falling short of the estimate I gave for their odds of success. I explain that there is a ***beginning, middle*** and ***end*** to a treatment process. The beginning is when we see any type of improvement in the pattern of symptoms, the middle is where we build on this and take it as far as possible, and the end is where we make sure the progress will be as stable and lasting as possible. Based on the response seen in the beginning stage, I will know better and inform them on what will likely happen in the middle and ending stages. I stress that it is difficult to know just how a patient will respond in the beginning. Some feel marked improvement from the very first treatment and move immediately into the middle stage. Others may take several treatments before showing even modest improvement. Patients that get off to a faster start usually end-up requiring less treatments overall and those who get off to a slower start usually end-up requiring more.

I will go into more detail about how I estimate all of the above a little later but to make matters simple here let me just say that I tell most of my patients that we should see some start of improvement within 5-6 treatments for most cases and then going up to perhaps 8-10 for the most difficult cases. I tell my prospective patients flat-out that if they want to try acupuncture, they need to be willing to give it at least those 5-6 treatments (or 8-10). Hopefully they will respond sooner than that, but to only try 2-3 treatments and quit if there is no improvement is not giving acupuncture a fair trial. I emphasize that I do not sell blocks of treatments and that they can of course stop treatment at any time, but doing less than those initial number of treatments is not being realistic. If we don't see the beginning of improvement by this number of treatments we will have to discuss the viability of further treatment because the odds that the treatment will eventually kick-in fall with each successive treatment.

Once we see improvement and are into the middle stage, that improvement should build steadily. As long as we see continued improvement, we should keep the treatments going until all the symptoms have subsided or the improvement plateaus. If the improvement plateaus before all the symptoms have subsided, we will need to have a talk about whether we have reached the maximum therapeutic benefit or if something different needs to be done to spark a new level of progress. I emphasize that it is not my policy to just keep treating if we are not seeing continued progress.

On that subject, I highly recommend that you do not get in the habit of doing what some acupuncturists (and chiropractors for that matter) do when they just keep treating until the patient decides to stop treatment. You should be monitoring their progress each step of the way and keep them informed as to how you see the treatment shaping-up. That is as much as anyone can do and once you explain all this to your patients during the initial intake, they will understand and appreciate that you are doing everything you can to keep them from wasting their time and money if the treatment is not progressing as initially estimated. If you just keep treating until the patient decides to stop, their satisfaction with your services will be lower than if you tell them that you believe you have taken them as far as possible and should stop the treatment. Your patients will be very impressed with this and their level of trust in you will be much higher as it reinforces that you have their best interest at heart. The same thing goes when estimating the odds of success. Telling a prospective patient that the odds the treatment will work for them are not good will impress your patients that you are honest and may actually generate more referrals than when you are successful. Honesty really is the best policy.

The protocol of taking the treatment in stages, frequently reviewing whether or not the patient is still progressing, and halting treatment once the maximum therapeutic benefit is reached is what I learned to do by trial and error in the first several years of my practice as I came to understand just what the market would bear. It is also the basic model used by most all insurance companies in one version or another, especially managed care plans. Managed care plans employ what is called "case management" or "utilization management" in which practitioners must justify the number and types of therapies they are requesting for their patients. This usually happens in stages with an initial series of treatments and then supplying information about the patient's progress to justify "medical necessity", i.e., that further treatment is necessary.

I mentioned being on the original panel of advisors to the insurance company American Specialty Health when they hired a dozen or so acupuncturists in 1996 to help them establish the guidelines they needed to bring A/OM services into the realm of managed care. This was the first (and perhaps only) time a large, diverse group of A/OM practitioners in the U.S. were brought together to work on such a project. Our advisory group consisted of experienced practitioners from different Asian and non-Asian educational backgrounds, many of whom were or had been leaders in A/OM organizations. We met regularly for over a year in marathon sessions sharing our perspectives and hashing-out differences. Despite the diverse backgrounds and different techniques employed by those participating in this, it was insightful to see that most everyone agreed on the basics of how many treatments it should take to see progress in successful cases and when one should be able to tell if the treatment was not being successful. While we all acknowledged there were exceptions, the consensus we reached on treatment (utilization) management was surprisingly universal. I was impressed by the directive we were given in beginning this work. We were told that the goal was to develop guidelines that would allow the approval of "not one more treatment than necessary and not one less treatment than necessary". Striving to strike that tricky balance between under-treating and over-treating was exactly how market realities had taught me to manage my practice and what I advise you to do also. If you think managed care utilization management policies are stingy, wait until you deal with cash patients. Nobody manages their care more closely than patients managing their own pocketbooks so you need to see that the treatments you recommend are necessary.

Chapter Recap:

1. **Offer a free initial consultation.**

2. **Gather information about the patient's pattern of symptoms.**

3. **Explain how acupuncture works in simple terms.**

4. **Estimate the odds that the treatment will be successful.**

5. **Focus the patient on how many treatments it should take to see the beginning of progress.**

6. **Explain that the treatment will be carried-out in stages: A beginning, a middle, and an end.**

7. **Explain that you will keep them informed during each stage of the treatment process and that you will not keep treating if it looks like the treatment is not working as expected or once the maximum therapeutic benefit is reached.**

CHAPTER EIGHT

Explaining How Acupuncture Works

I simply cannot stress enough how important it is for acupuncturists practicing in the West to be able to explain acupuncture to their patients. Acupuncture was born of a different culture and time and is traditionally explained using concepts such as qi, meridians, yin/yang or Five Elements that are so foreign to Westerners you might as well be trying to describe a healing system from another planet. The single greatest obstacle acupuncture has faced in the West is that its very premise—that you can help dozens of medical conditions by sticking solid needles in people, fiddle with them a bit, leave them in for a while, and then take them out—has no precedent in modern medical knowledge and defies mainstream Western logic. Add to that the fact that no one can prove that qi, meridians, or acupuncture points exist, and acupuncture is a very tough sell; or so one would think. After explaining acupuncture to thousands of people over many years and especially after writing a book that covered this topic, I finally figured out what I believe to be the best way to explain acupuncture so that it makes sense and allows my patients to understand just where they stand throughout the entire treatment process. Because explaining things in this manner is so fundamental to the relationship you will be able to build with your patients, I want to cover this topic in depth.

Acupuncturists often tell their patients that acupuncture works by helping the body to heal itself but few appreciate just how remarkable this simple fact is and why it must be stressed above all else when explaining acupuncture. Western medicine's strength is in its ability to intervene with strong, man-made resources that essentially are used to take over for the body and repair problems from the outside-in like a mechanic repairing a machine. The idea that you could have a medical system whose sole goal is to stimulate the body's own intrinsic resource—healing from the inside-out—has never been seriously considered in modern medicine so Western culture has no familiarity with such a concept.

The reason that acupuncture seems illogical to most Westerners is because they have never been subjected to a medical system that seeks to stimulate the body's internal resources. This is the biggest obstacle we face gaining credibility for acupuncture and we have been failing to recognize this. I believe we have been failing to do so because Chinese medicine is almost entirely based on helping the body to heal itself, so no one in the Far East bothered to contrast this approach with the opposite method of using outside resources. This being the case, acupuncture's early advocates in the West failed to point-out this all-important fundamental difference. If you try to understand how acupuncture works within a framework of helping the body from the outside-in, it makes no sense at all. That is why acupuncture was (and, in some circles, still is) met with such skepticism when it was introduced in the West. If you change the perspective however, and think of acupuncture as a treatment that seeks to heal from the inside-out by stimulating internal resources, it begins to make sense. As a matter of fact, by keeping this in mind, you can answer most every question people have about acupuncture.

In my book *"The Healing Power of Acupressure and Acupuncture"* I took some pains to describe the strengths and weaknesses of what I now call "Outside Medicine" and "Inside Medicine". In that book, I used the terms "Action Medicine" and "Reaction Medicine" for technical reasons but once I started doing radio interviews to promote that book, I realized the terms "Outside" and "Inside" medicine were more easily understood by the public. Again, most people in the West, both the public and medical authorities, think of medicine or any type of medical intervention only in terms of outside/mechanical medicine so acupuncturists need to be clear when speaking about acupuncture that we are dealing with a very different type of intervention. This takes some doing because most people have never thought of medicine in this way, but once you get them to understand that the entire focus of acupuncture is stimulating internal resources, you will see a light bulb go off in their head. They will literally tell you "That makes sense," and "Gee, I never thought about it that way before". You won't get that light bulb—that level of understanding—talking about qi.

A good example of how people have never been subjected to a medical system that stimulates internal resources can be seen in a common reaction some patients have when they are seen by an acupuncturist for the first time. Many times when I am explaining the treatment process to a new patient, a confused look comes over their face and they ask: "Is there medicine in the needles?" I like it when that happens because it gives me the chance to say: "No, the medicine is in your body. The needles help your body to make its own medicine." Then I see that light bulb go off. Now they understand. It seems like a strange idea to them, something they have never heard of from any doctor before but they have now had their biggest misunderstanding made clear and this allows us to be on the same page as we go along in their treatment process. Simple, isn't it?

Before I give you an example of how I go about explaining acupuncture as a system of inside medicine to a prospective patient, let's review this Inside Medicine concept as it is a novel approach for most acupuncturists and you may have doubts whether or not you agree with this basic premise.

Whenever I ask my fellow acupuncturists about how they think acupuncture works, I of course get explanations of balancing qi, freeing-up stuck qi, improving circulation, producing endorphins, stimulating neurotransmitters, activating key brain regulatory centers, etc., etc. I don't disagree with any of these explanations but these are like describing the details of specific trees instead of understanding the whole forest. When I speak of stimulating internal resources, I am stepping back and describing the forest itself. What are we doing when we balance qi but improving the efficiency of our internal resources? If acupuncture causes the production of endorphins or improves blood flow, aren't those internal resources? If acupuncture stimulates the limbic system of the brain isn't that area a vital component involved with how our organisms monitor and regulate our internal resources? There is not a single viable explanation of how acupuncture works that is not just another example of stimulating internal resources! Debating the different possible mechanisms of acupuncture is like debating the fact that there are different species of trees in a forest. The public needs to first be enlightened about the existence of this forest they were unaware of, not the details of the trees. This "big picture" perspective is compatible with whatever your personal detailed beliefs may be regarding how acupuncture works. It is also much easier for patients to understand. There is seldom a need to explain the details of the trees but if your patients ask, you can then explain about qi or endorphins or blood flow, etc.

I hope you are starting to see the advantage of using this type of explanation. To make it clearer, the following is an example of a typical explanation I give prospective patients once I have reviewed their current symptoms and history in their initial consultation:

"The most important thing I need to explain to you is that acupuncture works by helping the body to get more out of its own natural healing resources. Our bodies produce a wide range of natural pain relieving substances, natural anti-inflammatory chemistry, hormones, immune system enhancers, and so forth, all without the need for outside drugs. In fact, some of our most effective drugs are man-made synthetic copies of the chemistry our body makes naturally like cortisone. In modern medicine we made the mistake of assuming that when a problem lingers and is not healed right away by our internal natural resources, this must mean it is beyond our body's ability to heal. We then look to bring-in outside resources like drugs or surgery to address the problem. The fact is though, that just because a problem is not healed right away by our internal resources does not necessarily mean it is beyond those resources. We don't always get 100% from our inside self-healing resources anymore than we get 100% out of our brains' resources or our muscles' resources. Acupuncture helps us squeeze more out of our natural ability to heal ourselves—to get us closer to 100% of our full potential."

"Your body has already been trying to heal your problem but has not yet been able to get the upper hand on it. A good course of acupuncture treatment—done by someone well-trained in this system—should always be able to help anyone to improve their body's healing efforts by at least 10-20%. So what I need to try to figure-out in your case—like I try to do with all of my patients—is whether or not it seems likely getting you closer to 100% of your internal resources' potential by boosting those efforts 10-20% will make the difference needed to help your body to finish the job."

At this point most people will want to know how I am able to tell if their problem is of the type that will respond to a 10-20% boost. I then proceed to explain to them just how I can tell this, but before I go on to detail that process; let's review what I have said in my little speech above and why I phrased things in such a way.

Everybody knows that their body produces natural resources that heal many problems. If you get a paper cut on your finger for example, the body snaps into action and begins a surprisingly complex chain of events to repair this injury without the need for any man-made, outside medicine. But what if the cut is deeper? The body still snaps into action to try to repair this but a deep cut may be beyond those resources requiring a man made intervention such as stitches or even antibiotic drugs if the cut should get infected. In other words, there is a limit to the body's self-healing abilities and everyone can accept this with just a little explanation.

The crucial thing that acupuncturists need to explain is that not everyone gets 100% of their self-healing potential all the time and this being the case, just because a person's problem has lingered does not mean it is beyond their body's limits. A diabetic, for example, may have more difficulty healing a paper cut than a non-diabetic because of limits on their self-healing potential. Everybody, not just diabetics, have factors limiting their full potential to heal themselves. When I begin this line of explanation, I often see a bit of doubt in people's eyes when I suggest their problem might still be within their body's self-healing potential. They think if that were true, it should have repaired itself by now. When I then use the example of how people only use a fraction of their brain's potential at any given time, their doubt turns into a nod of understanding. Most everyone has heard that people don't use all of their brain cells or achieve their brain's full potential. By using this language, I am suggesting the hope that their health problem may yet be within their body's ability to manage is no more unreasonable than suggesting that they might be able to get a little more out of their brain's potential. Believe me; everybody thinks their brains could function better than they are. Using this type of explanation encourages people to hope that getting more out of their self-healing ability is no more far-fetched then hoping they could get more out of their brains ability.

I then go on to state that well-done acupuncture should consistently be able to give a good 10-20% boost to their resources. Note that I say it will take a "series of treatments" to spark this improvement because I want to start conditioning them to understand they need to give it several treatments before we can judge progress. I also mention this boost should happen if that series is done by a "well-trained" acupuncturist. I do that to establish that there is a difference between the skill level of all those out there doing acupuncture. This can be important as most people have no idea about the different levels of training that are required by different health-care providers to be able to legally perform acupuncture in the U.S. Finally, I use the very conservative figure of 10-20% boost in self-healing resources because it seems more plausible than higher figures and I would rather underestimate the potential than overestimate it. Why? Because if I low-ball the potential of the treatment and the patient is comfortable with starting treatment with modest expectations, they will be a better patient than if I sugar-coat everything and then have trouble achieving that. In other words, I would rather have my patients surprised and happy they exceeded expectations than surprised and disappointed they didn't achieve expectations.

The key to this approach is being able to figure-out if a 10-20% boost will make a difference for any given patient. I will explain my method for estimating the odds of success in the next chapter.

Chapter Recap:

1. **Stressing that acupuncture helps the body to heal/manage itself is the best way to describe how it works.**

2. **We seldom get 100% of our potential self-healing abilities.**

3. **Acupuncture helps us squeeze more out of our self-healing abilities.**

4. **A good course of acupuncture treatments done by a well-trained acupuncturist should consistently boost the self-healing efforts by 10-20%.**

5. **The best candidates for acupuncture are those in whom a 10-20% boost will allow the body to get the upper hand on the problem.**

CHAPTER NINE

Estimating the Odds of Success

When I speak of "estimating the odds of success", I am referring to how I go about explaining to my patients my best guess of whether they will benefit from the treatment. I will vary this explanation somewhat based on how I read each patient. For many, I literally give them odds in percentages with my highest percentage or best odds as 85-90% likelihood of success and the lowest odds at usually 30%. Other times, I just tell people I believe they have an excellent, very good, good, fair, or poor chance of doing well with the treatment. In a few cases, I don't bother being this specific because I get the picture that the patient is ready to begin the treatment without this information.

When you are dealing with a patient with an acute injury such as a sprained ankle, this is a condition that the body will be able to repair with time and the boost acupuncture gives should consistently be able to speed that recovery time. But with chronic conditions, there is far more uncertainty if acupuncture will make a significant difference. Acupuncture can certainly help a condition like asthma, but that does not mean you can tell every prospective asthma patient that acupuncture will be effective for them. Why is it that acupuncture can help one person with a condition like asthma but not everyone? How can you tell which ones the treatment will likely help and which ones are less likely? Most students are taught about assessing a patient by traditional diagnostic techniques such as pulse and tongue signs. While these techniques are important to understand the type of imbalance you are dealing with, there is a far simpler way to estimate the odds of success.

Because acupuncture works by boosting the body's efforts to heal/manage itself, the best candidate for this treatment is someone whose internal resources are very close to getting the problem under control and could do so with just a little boost. Estimating the odds of success then, is estimating whether or not giving a boost to a patient's internal resources will make a significant difference in their condition. Patients often can be helped in this way because many health problems are subject to "tipping points." The body is constantly struggling to manage continuous onslaughts to its homeostasis. When it starts to lose one of those struggles and a problem gets the upper hand, this is an example of the struggle "tipping" to the negative side. If the body's resources gain the upper hand and bring the problem under control, things have tipped to the positive side. Getting a reasonable idea of just how far a problem has progressed passed this tipping point is the crucial indicator of whether or not the boost acupuncture gives to the body will tip the struggle to the positive side.

The way you can get a good estimate of how far beyond such tipping points a given problem may be is by closely considering the pattern of your patient's symptoms. You especially want to learn about how consistent your patient's symptoms have been. Are the symptoms there 24/7 and stay the same no matter what the patient does or do the symptoms come and go? Does the patient have some good days when the symptoms don't bother them too much? If the symptoms are the same no matter what, that is a bad sign. If the symptoms fluctuate with some periods of little or no symptoms, this is a very good sign because it suggests the problem is close to the tipping point. In fact, I can pretty much tell if a patient is a good candidate for acupuncture by getting just one bit of information regardless of what type of condition they have or other factor like pulses, tongue signs, etc. All I need to find out is what range there is between his/her good, average, and bad level of symptoms. Say for example on a scale of 1-10 with ten being the worst suffering, a patient says their range of symptoms can go from a 2 to a 10 while a second one tells you their symptoms range from a 5 to a 6. Although having a 10 is worse than a 6, the patient with the range of a 2 to a 10 is actually a better candidate on average.

The example of the patient with symptoms ranging from a 2 to a 10 is the type of case where boosting the body's resources 10-20% will make a positive difference by allowing those resources to tip the scales to the positive side. But if a patient's symptoms consistently stay the same, especially if they have been staying that way for a long period of time, the boost acupuncture gives will be far less likely to tip things past this critical point. The treatment should always give the body a boost, but if the problem is dug-in well past the tipping point, the help this boost creates will not add up to much. By explaining things this way I am not saying acupuncture will always be successful in cases where the level of symptoms vary greatly and never be successful in those with little variation, I am saying the odds or probability of success are proportional to this variation. Let me state this again loud and clear:

"THE PROBABILITY OF SUCCESS WITH ACUPUNCTURE IS PROPORTIONAL TO THE VARIATION IN THE SEVERITY OF SYMPTOMS: THE GREATER THE VARIATION, THE GREATER THE PROBABILTIY OF SUCCESS."

Although few have thought of it in such stark terms as stated above, most experienced acupuncturists are quite familiar with the opposite of the above statement; the toughest cases are those who have had the same symptoms, with little variation, for the longest periods of time. This is true for virtually any type of problem from back pain to headaches to asthma to tinnitus. Name the condition and the pattern is the same. This is what is so beautiful about practicing inside medicine; we don't have to know everything about every condition—*we just have to know how to squeeze more out of the body's resources and how to weigh the probability that this boost will make a worthwhile difference.* If you can be successful in those two things, you will help thousands of people in your career and have a much better chance of building a successful practice.

I can even make it much simpler for you by suggesting a reliable short-cut that will allow you to tell a potential patient if your treatments have a good chance for success. Another way to approach the variation in symptoms is to ask your potential patient the difference between their good, average, and bad days. I tell my patients that a series of acupuncture treatments should consistently be able to shift everyone one notch in the better direction. Ask them: "If I could make your average days be like your good days are now, would you be happy with that?" If the range in their symptoms is great like the 2-10 example, their answer will be "yes" and you can tell them with confidence that they should be a very good candidate for treatment (70-80%). If the range is small, the answer will likely be "no" and you can let them know that the odds are not so good for them (40-50%). There are many caveats to framing things in this way that will impact those odds and we will consider these but this short-cut is quite accurate in most cases and also helps your patients better understand the treatment process. Many patients will tell you that they are not expecting a miracle cure—they are just hoping for some relief from their symptoms. If there is reasonable space between their good, average, and bad range, shifting them a notch in the better direction should give them that relief.

Don't worry too much about your confidence in being able to give accurate measurements of the odds of success. It is just an initial estimate and people will understand that you are trying to give them your best guess. While my years of experience have helped me better gauge these odds, most of this guess work is based on some logical principals I will try to explain here. The number one and most important is the one already mentioned; the degree of variation of the symptoms. Others include:

2.) The length of time those symptoms have persisted.
3.) The overall health of the patient.
4.) The age of the patient.
5.) Other medical problems they may have.
6.) Medications they may be on (including recreational drug/alcohol use).

While the most weight needs to be placed on the level of variation in the pattern of symptoms—the length of time of that pattern is the second most important factor. The other co-factors are roughly equal but less significant than these first two. Someday I may actually try to develop a matrix tool where these factors are more carefully weighted to give a formal estimate of the odds but for now let me just describe these factors in terms of general rules of thumb.

As mentioned above, what needs to be assessed is the degree beyond a problem's tipping point. The tipping point was passed when the patient first became aware of the symptoms. If the patient tells you that on the 1-10 scale the problem bounces back and forth from a 7 back to a 1 or 2, this strongly suggests their system is very near being able to bring the problem under control and the modest boost acupuncture should give will make a significant positive difference. These cases should rate a solid 75-85% probability of success if the co-factors are reasonably favorable.

If factor number 2—the length of time the patient has had the same pattern of symptoms—is relatively longer, this will make the odds a little less favorable. If this pattern of symptoms has been persisting for 6 weeks for example, that would not reduce the probability of success while having that same pattern for 6 years would. How much? Perhaps 1% or 2% a year. Again, this is just a gross estimate based on my experience but you should find this system fairly reliable. If the other co-factors are negative, they can each reduce the probability of success somewhere on the order of 3-5%.

For example, say you gather information on a prospective patient's pattern of symptoms (detailed later) and they tell you these symptoms can some days be as high as a 7 or on others can be gone completely or at most a 1 or 2. Remember, as a practical, rough guideline, it makes almost no difference what the medical condition may be—what matters is the pattern of symptoms. You then find out how long this pattern has been happening and make note of their overall health, age, other medical problems, and medications. If they have only had this pattern of symptoms for a few months or less, are in good overall health, are not elderly, don't have any other specific medical problems, and are not on medications, then their odds of success should be a solid 75% or even more. Someone forty-years-old who has poor general health, several medical problems and taking several medications would have somewhat lower odds than someone seventy years old in good health with no other medical conditions or medications.

If the symptoms vary a large amount, the odds of success should be at least 50/50 and usually better depending on the other factors. If the symptoms don't vary much but the problem is a recent one, there is still a good chance the treatment will be successful depending on the type of problem you are dealing with. If you know you are dealing with a type of problem that the body's resources cannot put a dent in, then the fact the problem's onset was recent does not help the odds. When I speak of the variation in the symptoms, I am referring to how much they vary when subjected to the same influencing factors. The symptoms of someone with allergies for example will vary a lot between when they are exposed to their triggering allergen versus when they are not. The variation I am referring to would be if they have a noticeable variation in their symptoms when exposed to the same allergens. Someone with low back pain may tell you that when they sit they have no pain but as soon as they stand the pain is a 10. That variation does not count. If they tell you the pain when they stand is sometimes a 10 and others a 2 that counts and is a good sign they are near the tipping point.

If you don't have a lot of confidence in your ability to use percentages you can use the other system of measuring I mentioned: Excellent, very good, good, average, poor. You just want to give the patient some realistic estimate to get things started and then refine that based on how your patients respond during the first phase of the treatment process. Or you can use the *good*, *average*, and *bad* range of symptoms approach. Just give them some kind of estimate, based on the particulars of their pattern of symptoms rather than a using a generic list of conditions acupuncture can supposedly treat.

Chapter recap:

1. **Many health problems are subject to tipping points where just a little boost will help the body get the upper hand on a problem.**

2. **Estimating the odds of success is estimating if the 10-20% boost acupuncture gives will tip the struggle to the positive side.**

3. **The best gauge for estimating if a problem is near the tipping point is the degree of variation in the pattern of symptoms; the greater the variation the better the odds.**

4. **Other important considerations for estimating the odds of success are:**
   The length of time those symptoms have persisted.
   The overall health of the patient.
   The age of the patient.
   Other medical conditions.
   Medications including recreational drug/alcohol use.

5. **You can estimate the odds of success using percentages or a scale of good, fair, poor, etc.**

6. **A reliable short-cut is to find out if making the patient's average day be like their present good day would be valuable to them.**

CHAPTER TEN

Focus on the Initial Series of Treatments and the Five and Ten Rule

Estimating the odds of success in the manner just described is done during the initial consultation to give your patient some sort of reasonable idea of what they can expect from the treatment. As I mentioned before, when you give these odds, you need to emphasize that this is just your best guess at this stage. You will get a better idea how the treatment is doing during the initial series of treatments because the treatments are both therapeutic and diagnostic. Once you see how they are responding to this initial series of treatments, you will keep them informed of your revised estimate of the odds; whether or not they seem to be meeting, exceeding or falling short of your original estimate. Explaining things in this manner begins the process of shifting a prospective patient's focus away from the question of how many treatments may be needed in the end to how many it should take in the beginning to see any progress.

As mentioned earlier, you can't know how many treatments it will take in the end because there are too many factors beyond your control that will influence the outcome. Even if your estimate of this turns out to usually be correct, you're better off not focusing the patient on that number at the start because it might discourage them from beginning the treatment. Say, for example, you are seeing a prospective patient who has been suffering from migraine headaches for ten years and your best guess is that it will take 20 treatments over the next four months to reach the maximum therapeutic benefit that will bring the headaches under control and you charge $50 P/T. Your prospective patient will do the math and look at it like they are being asked to commit to spending a thousand dollars without any guarantee of success. Many will balk at that commitment. But if you tell them they should see improvement within the first 5-6 treatments and that this improvement should grow with each mini-series of treatments, then they are only committing to $250-$300 to see if they may able to get help for their problem and they know they can stop before then if they don't feel comfortable with how things are going.

It is difficult for most people to imagine how acupuncture will help them until they start actually experiencing the benefits. This being the case, they will not be able to accurately gauge the value of the treatment until then. Once they are improving they can judge for themselves if they think the treatment charge is worth it. I have had many patients end-up coming to me for more treatments than they would have thought at first because they could not measure the value of the treatments until they experienced the benefits. You just need to get your foot in the door with your patients in other words and then do everything you can to deliver enough of a perceived benefit at a reasonable cost in a pleasant environment so that your patients can experience the benefits and appreciate the value of your services.

A majority of patients should see improvement within the first 5-6 treatments. That is fortunate because that number also happens to be roughly the maximum number most people will give these treatments before stopping if they do not perceive any benefit. Interestingly, this tends to be the case if they are paying cash for the entire treatment charge, only a small co-payment with insurance, or even if they have no out-of-pocket expense under a Workers Compensation or Personal Injury case. This is also roughly the number of treatments HMO plans will want to see improvement by before authorizing further treatments. I refer to this phenomenon as part of what I call the "*Five* and *Ten*" rule.

The number five in the *Five* and *Ten* rule is roughly the number most people will give the treatment in the beginning and ten is about how long they will go in the end if they are seeing improvement. This being the case, my advice is that for most of your patients, you had better be able to provide at least some perceived benefit within 5 treatments and be well on the way to providing substantial benefit by 10 treatments. You should be able to do this with a high percentage of patients whose pattern of symptoms suggests that their condition is near the tipping point as discussed previously. You may get a little more chance out of some patients—say six and twelve—but you should shoot for succeeding in the five and ten treatment framework to better your chances.

Some cases, however, cannot be expected to respond within 5-6 treatments. A patient with neuropathy who has had complete numbness in both legs from the knees to their feet for 10 years has a low probability of success because their symptoms have had little variation for a long period of time. You could rate this type of case at maybe 30%-40% depending on those other factors of general health, age, etc. In this type of case, you could tell the prospective patient those odds and let them know that if they wanted to try the treatment, they should be prepared to give it at least 8-10 treatments. Anything less would not be giving it a reasonable chance. Again, you need to stress that such estimates are just initial estimates and that there is always a chance that they might beat those odds. The only way to tell is to start treating.

While this type of estimate doesn't sound too promising, you don't want to sugar-coat things and then end-up with a disappointed patient when you can't deliver. It is a better policy to keep your estimates on the conservative side. If a patient decides to start treatment with a conservative estimate of success, then he/she will be happy if you do better. While you might think someone that has been given the odds mentioned in the hypothetical neuropathy case above would never try the treatment, a surprising number will. Many of the patients who have these poor odds will have been told by their doctors that there is nothing that can be done for them. A 30% chance is still better than no chance at all. And when you practice a therapy that works by giving a boost to the body's internal resources, you honestly never know when you might surpass the average odds (just as you don't know when you may fall short). Just be honest with your patients. They will respect that.

The purpose of the initial trial of treatments is to better understand whether or not the patient's condition is responsive to stimulating their internal resources. While every practitioner needs to develop his/her own protocol for assessing this based on his/her style of practice, we can learn a great deal by considering how acupuncture treatments have been done in China in the recent past. A good deal of acupuncture was performed in hospital and large clinic settings under a fully socialized system where there was virtually an unlimited number of treatments that could be done to give that form of therapy every chance of success. A very helpful resource that sheds light on how acupuncture was used in that system is a book published by Eastland Press titled "*Acupuncture Case Histories from China*". As the title implies, this book is a collection of cases in several different areas of medicine—internal medicine, neurology, dermatology, etc.—that describes the treatment process used in each case.

In this book, a description is given of the results of the treatment process and describes how most chronic conditions were treated every other day and that a "course" of treatments would consist of 10-15 treatments. While many cases describe improvement taking place within the first few treatments, some describe cases requiring two or more courses of treatments (20-30 treatments or more) before an improvement takes place. This book provides detailed accounts of some cases requiring dozens of treatments trying different treatment strategies before the first sprout of improvement was noticed. Most cases described in this book, however, responded with far fewer treatments.

My point in explaining what is detailed in this book is that while it may be true that improvement sometimes first begins only after a large number of treatments are done, the vast majority of cases respond within a more modest number—usually within 5-10 treatments. This is what you need to make clear to your patients. It is impossible to say that if 5-10 treatments are tried and no improvement takes place that this means no improvement could ever happen with any number of treatments. However, the odds that any improvement will happen get worse with each passing treatment beyond the initial 5-10. Unlike a fully socialized medical system, in private practice we don't have the luxury of unlimited treatments and so we need to be vigilant about accessing when the odds have gotten so poor that continuing treatment is likely pointless. Of course, if you explain all this and a patient tells you they can afford it and they want to keep trying, that is fine—keep trying different techniques and keep your fingers crossed. Every once in a while, that type of persistence will pay-off and that's great. But if trying more and more treatments does not yield results; at least you did your job by being honest about the odds and your patients will respect you for that.

Chapter Recap:

1. Focus the patient on the initial series of treatments.

2. Acupuncture is both therapeutic and diagnostic.

3. Once you see how the patient is responding to the initial series of treatments you can revise your original estimate of the odds of success.

4. It is difficult for patients to appreciate the value of acupuncture until they start experiencing the benefits.

5. Most patients will experience improvement within the first 5-6 (or 8-10) treatments.

6. Do your best to make some improvement happen within the first 5-6 treatments and to build improvement over the subsequent 5-6 treatments.

7. It is better to underestimate the odds of success than over-estimate them.

CHAPTER ELEVEN

How to Get the Information You Need

In order to get the information I need to estimate the odds of success, the first thing I will ask my patients during the initial consultation is to describe for me their *current* symptoms. I tell them I will find out about the history of their problems next but it helps me the most to first know just what they are experiencing on a daily basis now. I don't yet want to know what their doctor told them or what happened to them 20 years ago or to look at any lab tests or MRI reports—*I first only want to know what symptoms they are having that brought them to my office.* This would seem like a simple request, but it often goes in one ear and out the other before they launch into their life stories. Sometimes you have to go along with this for a bit but I suggest you work on your approach for getting new patients to focus on giving you a run-down of their current symptoms first because everything else you do will proceed from there. This information should have been indicated to some degree on the intake form they filled-out but you still want them to describe this to you verbally.

There are two important reasons you want to get an accurate description of your new patients' current symptoms. First, as mentioned above, you want to gauge what the odds are that the boost acupuncture gives their internal resources will have a positive impact on their condition. To do this you want to know the degree or variation of their symptoms as well as other details I will explain shortly. The other reason for getting an accurate description of their symptoms is so you can establish baseline starting points against which you will measure ongoing progress. I will go into detail describing my protocol for measuring progress as this can be crucial to how you manage your patients, especially in helping them perceive early benefit.

Once your patient tells you just what symptoms he/she is experiencing, get enough details so you know you are both on the same page. A patient may tell you about pain in the "hip" but is it really in the hip joint (GB30) area or the posterior iliac crest area (Bl53)? When appropriate, have your patient point out for you just where in their body the problem is; don't just take his/her description using anatomical terms. Next ask if there is anything that tends to make these symptoms feel better or worse. This is a very important question because it relates to the degree of variation in their symptoms. For musculoskeletal type problems for example, ask how the symptoms behave when they are standing, sitting, walking, or lying down. For digestive disorders ask how their symptoms react when they eat, move their bowels, have an empty stomach, etc. *You are looking for anything that causes changes in the pattern of symptoms because this information yields the most useful insights regarding the nature of their problems including the tipping points.* This will help you to both estimate the odds of success and measure their progress.

Sara and Jim

For example: A patient—let's call her "Sara"—tells you she has terrible, constant pain in her hip. You ask her to point out to you just where she means and she points to her right Bl53 area. You then ask if the pain is there all the time or does it come and go? She tells you it is constant, it is there every day. You then ask if it is the same throughout the day: morning, noon, and night? She tells you it hurts a lot when she first gets up in the morning, eases in the later morning and early afternoon, and then starts to bother her more again by evening time. You then ask if the level of pain is the same every day and she tells you that on some days the pain is not too bad but she has at least some pain every day.

Notice in this example that the details you get after asking specific questions are different from what the patient first told you: She didn't have pain in the hip joint and her pain, while daily, is not consistent.

Now you should ask her how her pain reacts when doing common activities such as walking, sitting, standing, and lying down. She tells you it feels okay when she sits or lies down but standing or walking bothers her. Ask for more details: Does it hurt when you first stand or walk or only after you have been standing or walking for a long time? She tells you it is okay at first but bothers after standing or walking for a while. You then need to ask just how long she can typically stand or walk before it bothers her. Does it bother her after standing 1 minute, 5 minutes, 20 minutes, one hour? Can she walk 20 feet before it bothers or 1 block or one mile?

Let's say she tells you that she can stand for 10-15 minutes before the pain bothers her and walk for maybe one block. You then ask what happens if she has to stand or walk a long time and she says the pain gets really bad. You then should ask if when she sits or lies down, will the pain ease quickly or will it take several minutes or hours to ease or will it hurt for days after an episode like that? She tells you once it gets really aggravated she has to sit or lie down for a few hours for it to ease again.

Now—and only now—do you have some idea of just what Sara's symptoms actually are. She is not a patient with constant hip joint pain, she is someone with pain in the right posterior iliac area that wakes with some moderate pain and stiffness that eases with light activity then starts to bother her more by the end of the day. She can sit or lie down without aggravating the pain but can only stand or walk a modest amount before causing an exacerbation lasting a few hours. You will want to note these details as part of the intake information so that you can refer back to them during the initial treatment series as I will describe in Chapter Thirteen.

Sara's symptoms are different from another patient—let's call him "Jim"—who, like Sara, tells you he has daily pain in his right posterior iliac crest area. When you question Jim further, however, he tells you his pain is constant with little variation in the morning, noon, or night whether or not he is walking, sitting, standing, or lying down. The odds of success in treating Sara are much better than for Jim. This does not mean you can tell Sara her odds for success are 100% and that Jim's odds for success are 0% but it does mean you are dealing with two different types of cases even though they would seem to be very similar on the surface. You should go on to ask Jim the same questions you asked Sara about the details of his current pattern of symptoms.

Once you have a clear picture of the current pattern of symptoms your patient has, you are now ready to ask about the history of those symptoms. When would they say the symptoms just described first began? It is best to frame that question in that way; you don't want to hear about the whiplash they had 20 years ago or when they fell on the playground and hurt their tailbone 40 years ago. At this point in your intake process, you want to know how long ago it was that the very pattern of symptoms you just teased-out of them first began. Sara tells you these symptoms first began 4-5 months ago and Jim tells you his symptoms began 10 years ago.

You have established the pattern of symptoms that brought these patients into your office and when these symptoms first began. You should now ask if there was a specific incident that brought on these symptoms: Was there an accident of some sort, a fall or an auto accident? Did these symptoms just kind of happen with no known reason? Sara tells you her pain just started with no known injury while Jim tells you his pattern of symptoms began after he had lumbar disc surgery following a fall from a ladder. The odds are looking better for Sara and worse for Jim.

Once you have the above information, you can ask about whether or not they have been seen by any other health care provider for this problem. Have they been to a medical doctor, chiropractor, physical therapist? Were there any tests run such as X-Rays, MRI, CT scans? If so, what were the outcomes of these tests? Do they have a copy of any radiology reports describing the findings of these tests? If so, you want a copy of these for your records and you can look those over to see what the findings were. If they don't have copies of these reports, what did the doctor tell them about what the tests revealed? What diagnosis did the doctor reach? Are they on any medications for this condition or doing any physical therapy or home exercises?

Sara tells you that her medical doctor did X-rays and told her she had arthritic degeneration. He gave her muscle relaxers and anti-inflammatory medications but when they did not help, he sent her to physical therapy but that did not help either. You then need to ask Sara what the physical therapists did with her. She tells you they started doing hot packs and some machine they rubbed on her (ultrasound) and light massage then later had her doing exercises and did stronger massage on her. None of this helped so they discharged her and gave her exercises to do at home and her doctor told her that there is no cure for the degeneration and she needs to keep doing the exercises to stay as active as possible and he prescribed her some pain medication. Sara tells you she knows the acupuncture can't cure her arthritis but hoped it might be able to help with the pain some as she does not like to take the pain medication due to the side-effects.

At this point you need to ask Sara to try to remember as best she can what her symptoms were like when she first began P.T. and if they changed when her exercises were started. She tells you—now that she thinks about it—that her pain was not quite as bad at first and that, if anything, she got worse once she started the exercises. **BINGO.** Sara's symptoms are not being caused by arthritic degeneration. The pattern of symptoms does not fit the pattern that would happen if arthritic degeneration were the cause. *If arthritic degeneration were the sole cause, she would not have much variation in her symptoms as the degeneration does not vary.* Sara more than likely has suffered some soft-tissue strain, i.e. minor tearing of muscle/tendon fibers that was aggravated by the exercises prescribed by the physical therapist. Sara's pattern of symptoms and history suggest a high probability of success – 75%-85% likelihood she will have complete or near complete recovery with acupuncture treatment.

Jim, on the other hand, is looking like a much tougher case. He has been in constant pain with little variation since his lumbar surgery. You ask Jim whether or not he ever discussed his situation with his surgeon and he tells you his surgeon said the surgery was successful and he thought the pain he was having after the surgery was probably from scar tissue and that there was nothing that could be done for that. Since that time he has been seen by a few different doctors and tried physical therapy, chiropractic, pain meds, and had a few spinal injections. The pain meds take a slight edge off the pain and the first injection reduced the pain for a few weeks or so but later ones did nothing.

The unfortunate fact is that in Jim's case, you cannot be sure just what is causing his pain. It is most likely not scar tissue as Jim had this pain too soon following surgery. It is just as likely that the surgery caused some damage. In Jim's case—as with all cases—you are trying to figure-out if stimulating his internal resources will make a difference by allowing his body to get the upper hand on the problem. Unlike Sara's case, in which there was no history of an injury that could have caused damage beyond the body's ability to repair and her symptoms show a fairly large degree of variation, Jim's symptoms followed surgery that can cause irreparable damage and his symptoms have a long pattern of very little variation.

So what do you tell Jim? Do you tell him there is no use in even trying the treatment because it will just be a waste of time and money or do you keep your doubts to yourself and tell Jim how effective acupuncture often is for low back pain and begin treating him hoping to beat the odds? My advice is that, like the neuropathy example I gave earlier, you tell Jim that, in your opinion, the odds that the treatment will be successful are not good—maybe a 30-40% chance or so but that what you advise is an initial series of 8-10 treatments to see how he responds.

In Sara's case, I would tell her that she should see some improvement within the first 5-6 treatments. When I say this, I am not making a prediction that Sara won't see any improvement until the 5th or 6th treatment or Jim until the 8th through 10th treatment, I am saying that it could take that long but if we see no improvement by those numbers, it is a bad sign that the treatment may not work at all. Both Sara and Jim might feel improvement after the very first treatment but it is impossible to know which patients will get off to a faster start and which ones will take longer. If Sara does not show any improvement after 6 treatments or Jim after 10, I will have a talk with them about whether or not it makes sense to keep trying or if we should stop at that point.

In my examples of Sara and Jim, I used examples of musculoskeletal type problems because they are so common and lend themselves to considering how to ask probing questions regarding variations in symptoms. The basic strategy described above also applies to other types of conditions. You are looking for and taking note of tipping points, those factors that make the patterns of symptoms vary.

Chapter Recap:

1. **First get an account of your patient's current symptoms to estimate the odds of success and establish a baseline to measure progress against.**

2. **Ask if anything makes the symptoms better or worse—anything that changes the pattern of their symptoms.**

3. Find out the pattern of symptoms throughout the day—morning, noon and night.

4. Ask how long ago the symptoms just described first began.

5. Find out how this condition first began and whether there was a specific incident that set it off or it just came on gradually with no known reason.

6. Ask if they have seen other health care providers for this problem and what was the outcome of that?

7. Consider the possibility that previous medical care may have aggravated the problem.

CHAPTER TWELVE

Spacing Treatments to Get the Most From the Least

During my A/OM schooling my most influential teacher was a Korean doctor who had been in practice for more than 20 years. The first day I came to train at his clinic, he told me some advice his teacher had given him when he was just starting out: "Save the very best point for the last treatment." Coming from a background of working in construction, I was familiar with this way of thinking. In construction the old-timers will warn the young bucks about working too fast calling it: "Working yourself out of a job." While not working yourself out of a job by saving the best point for the last treatment may have been good business advice 50 years ago in Korea, I don't recommend that approach to practice building in the West today. The best way to make it in private practice today is by learning how to get the most benefit out of the least number of treatments.

When I first opened my practice, I made the mistake of trying to schedule my patients' treatments in such a way as to get the maximum improvement in the least amount of time. This is what is done in the TCM hospital clinics in China and was what I had been taught and observed in my school's clinic. Although this approach would seem to be the smartest way to proceed it is often not the best one to take within a private practice setting. Why? Because there is a difference between how to help your patients the fastest and how to help them the most with the least number of treatments. You should assume your patients prefer to get better cheaper rather than faster. Let me say that again: ***ASSUME YOUR PATIENTS PREFER TO GET BETTER CHEAPER RATHER THAN FASTER.*** Since the number of treatments is directly proportional to the ultimate costs of your services, you should try to get the most improvement with the least number of treatments. There are some exceptions of course but assuming that your patients' preference is to squeeze the most benefit out of the least cost is the best way to proceed in the vast majority of cases.

Most of the patients who seek-out acupuncture are suffering from chronic problems and even if they aren't, the majority of your patients will require several treatments to get the most benefit from your service. This being the case, how you time or space your treatments is every bit as important as what you do during the treatments. Suppose, for example, you have a fixed number of treatments–say 10–that will be all you get to use to try to help someone suffering from frozen shoulder. How will you space these treatments? Will you see the patient every day for 10 days? Will you see them once a week for 10 weeks or twice a week for 5 weeks? How you space treatments has a major impact on the outcome and learning how to get the most from the least is a vital skill that will significantly affect your ability to deliver your services with the greatest value for your patients.

Of course, unless you are dealing with an insurance plan that has a set limit in the maximum number of treatments allowed and your patient lets you know up front that they will not keep coming for treatment once that limit is reached, you rarely have a situation where you know for certain you have a fixed number of treatments to work with. What I learned from years of practice, however, is that even though there is nothing formally limiting the number of treatments you have to work with, market realities impose such limits. In other words, in private practice there ultimately *is* a set number of treatments you will have to work with but you won't know what that number is when you start treatment. I touched on this in the section on estimating the number of treatments it will take to see the first signs of improvement—my *Five and Ten* rule. Your patients, however, will not have thought this out before beginning the treatment process so they won't warn you in advance. They also often won't tell you when they are about ready to stop treatment. They tend instead to just stop coming without a word, maybe call your office saying they need to cancel their next appointment with you and that they will call you back to schedule another one but then never call back. While it may be possible to convince a patient who stopped coming-in for treatment to return for more treatment, you really want to do all you can to prevent this from happening.

In the recent years, some senior A/OM practitioners in the U.S. have commented on this issue of how to space treatments noting that most acupuncturists here treat at once a week while in the hospitals and clinics in China treatment is usually done daily or every other day. Some of these authorities advise treating three times a week to reduce the back-sliding that can occur when you stretch treatments out too far. While I certainly agree with the basic premise that spacing treatments out too far is less efficient, I personally think treating three times a week runs the risk of being too expensive for many patients that require treatment over an extended period of time. Even if money is not a problem, more frequent treatment becomes a strain on your patients' time and ultimately causes them to end the treatment process earlier than they otherwise would have. Treating daily or every other day can be best for recent, acute conditions that will only require a few treatments but for chronic conditions needing a longer period of time to treat, getting the most from the least by proper treatment spacing is critical.

I start off most of my patients at two treatments a week for the first 2-3 weeks and then go down to once a week for maybe 4-5 weeks after that depending on circumstances. At a minimum, I try to get new patients to begin with 3 treatments within the first 7-9 days. As I explained above, many patients will stop treatment if they don't see results within the first 5-6 treatments and often have a maximum of around 10-12 treatments. If you start them off at three times a week, you only have two weeks to get progress started and about three weeks before your patient is approaching 10 treatments. While this approach can work fine for some patients, it runs the risk of burning through a patient's limit of money or time before that first sprout of progress appears.

A key aspect to my protocol is trying to get a similar level of benefit out of two treatments per week normally expected from three treatments a week. Doing this can make a big difference in the *Five and Ten* rule. In addition to spacing the treatments as just described, another way I do this is to place emphasis on what the patient does in between the treatments—on elements of self-care. I want my patients to do all they can to both aid the treatment I am undertaking and especially to avoid things that could reduce the progress the treatments are beginning to generate. Educating my patients on how they can help me to help them is one of the most important aspects to my strategy of squeezing the most benefit out of the least number of treatments in order to have the best chance of producing a perceived benefit at a manageable cost. I will cover the topic of patient self-care in Chapter Fourteen.

Sparking and Riding Momentum

In the section on my protocol for the intake process I stated that you should explain to your patients that the treatment takes place in three sections—beginning, middle, and end. There is a momentum to the treatment process that often builds during the middle stage. Spacing your treatments so you can spark this momentum and then ride it with the fewest number of treatments is another critical element to squeezing the most from the least. Schedule twice-weekly treatments to get the first bit of improvement started and continue at that pace to push that momentum in the first part of the middle stage. Once you have this momentum, you can reduce the treatments to once a week for the remainder of the middle stage, riding the momentum until nearing the maximum therapeutic benefit. How do you know if you are reaching the maximum therapeutic benefit? In some cases this will happen when the symptoms completely disappear. In others there may be an aspect of the problem that is beyond the body's resources so some of the problem will remain. To know if you are at the ending stage you should stretch the last 2-3 treatments out to every 2 or even 3 weeks. If the symptoms begin to return when you stretch this way, you had not yet reached the ending stage and you need to do a few more treatments at once a week. If the progress reached up to this point holds, you can release the patient from your care.

You will also find some cases where the symptoms could be made to completely resolve but it is impractical to keep treating until this happens. These are cases where the momentum of progress has slowed but is still taking place a little at a time. In these cases when you reduce treatment to once every 2-3 weeks, there is still gradual improvement. That is a good sign and you can stop treatment and let your patient know that they should continue to see gradual improvement for several weeks afterward even though treatment has been stopped. This happens because some problems take a very long time before reaching the maximum therapeutic benefit but don't need continual treatment to reach this due to momentum.

As I emphasized earlier, understanding that acupuncture sparks the body's internal resources helps explain virtually every aspect of how acupuncture works. This includes the phenomena of momentum in self-healing. When one is beginning to spark these resources with the first treatments, the improvement this brings is often limited and short lived because the body has fallen into some bad habits in how it utilizes those resources. The qi flow has become restricted and/or diverted to some errant pathways. The longer the qi has been affected this way, the more it gets worn into that errant flow. Like water, qi follows the path of least resistance and so tends to flow in a "follow-the-leader" habit. Effective acupuncture helps shift the flow back into the proper pathways, but until those proper pathways become as well-worn as the errant pathways, the qi will keep following the wrong path. Once the proper pathways become well-worn and less restrictive than the errant pathways, the qi will naturally follow this course without the need for continual pushes from the treatment. Experienced acupuncturists can actually sense this unfolding during the treatment process although no one can exactly predict this all the time.

Everything in nature is a creature of habit because qi is a creature of habit. It takes time for bad qi flow habits to form and it takes time for good habits to be restored. Fortunately, the deck is usually stacked in our favor as nature is inclined to have normalcy. If we can just give the right kind of push often enough to help restore this normal flow, things should take care of themselves. That is what is so beautiful about facilitating self-healing. Being able to do this with acupuncture is a valuable skill. Being able to do this with the least number of treatments and the least out-of-pocket costs adds layers of complexity to this skill but is critical to private practice success. Spacing the treatments as described above should help you accomplish this.

As a rough rule of thumb, I have found that there is a basic ratio in how to space treatments to get the most out of the least by understanding how to take advantage of momentum. As a general rule, the number of weeks you treat at once a week should be about double of those weeks you treated at twice a week. If it takes treating a patient twice a week for three weeks to get momentum started, then treating them once a week for six weeks should get them through the middle stage to maximum therapeutic benefit. If treating twice a week for two weeks gets the momentum started then once a week for four weeks should be about right for the next stage. For those difficult cases that might need twice a week for five weeks to get the momentum started they will probably require once a week for ten weeks to near the maximum therapeutic benefit. This is why you need to see how the patient responds in the first stage to have an idea of how many treatments it may take after that. And as the number of treatments it takes in the end tends to be proportional to how many treatments it took to get the momentum started in the beginning it is important to do all you can to get that momentum rolling with the least number of treatments in the beginning stage.

Cost Concerns

Some of your patients will tell you that they can't afford to do any more than once a week treatment. There are several different ways you can approach this. One way is to just treat them once a week and hope for the best. What I usually do, however, is to stress that the approach I have suggested is meant to get the very best progress with the least number of treatments and that if we space the treatments out too far in the beginning, it runs the risk of not getting the momentum going in the early stages. This in turn could end up taking more treatments in the end or perhaps not be effective at all. I remind them that toward the end stage of the three stage treatment process we would be stretching to once every two or three weeks. I suggest that they come in twice a week—at very least three times in the first 7-9 days—but just pay me for one treatment per week and we will carry the balance over until the end stage when they are being seen less than once a week. Of course, you could always offer a discount or throw in some treatments for no charge but this sometimes backfires as many don't like to be made to feel like a charity case. Offering to let them pay off the balance at the end stage both helps keep your fee per treatment average in your target range and allows the patient to not feel too awkward about being given charity. It also emphasizes that you are trying to do everything you can to squeeze the most for the least and that wins the trust of your patients.

The problem of not being able to afford twice weekly treatments in the beginning stages is much more of an issue for those who do not have any insurance. By accepting insurance, you should be able to lower this problem significantly. I will discuss the issue of accepting insurance in Chapter Seventeen.

Chapter Recap:

1. Assume your patients would rather get better cheaper than faster and space treatments accordingly to squeeze the most benefit from the least number of treatments.

2. Start your patients at two treatments a week (3-4 days between treatments) for the first 2-3 weeks or at least 3 treatments in the first 7-9 days.

3. Reduce to once weekly treatments for the next 4-5 weeks or double the number used in twice weekly treatment.

4. Try to get the benefit of three treatments a week with only two treatments a week by educating patients on elements of self-care.

5. When it seems the treatment has reached maximum therapeutic benefit, reduce to every 2-3 weeks to check for backsliding.

6. If backsliding occurs, go back to once weekly treatment and then repeat above once it seems maximum therapeutic benefit has been reached.

CHAPTER THIRTEEN

Measuring Progress in The Four Factors (Plus One)

In the section on how to get the information you need, I discussed the types of questions you should ask your patient about their current pattern of symptoms so that you can establish a baseline against which you will measure their future progress. I also mentioned that people tend to be poor observers of their own progress especially when that progress takes place by virtue of stimulating their internal resources. In this section, I want to detail my protocol for measuring progress. Measuring progress is also another important aid to squeezing the most benefit out of the least number of treatments. A good percentage of patients feel marked improvement early-on in the treatment process. In those cases you have already cleared the first and biggest hurdle of making the first sprout of improvement appear and are now in the middle stage of building on that progress. Other patients don't get off to such a good start, however, and so there is pressure to spark some perceived benefit before those first 5 or 6 treatments are used.

There are four specific factors to a patient's pattern of symptoms I look to measure and a fifth consideration that can have an effect on these four. The first of these four is the one your patients will focus on most and that is the ***intensity*** of the symptoms. In conditions involving pain, the intensity can be measured on a 1-10 scale for example. For conditions that don't involve pain, it may not be quite as easy to put a number on intensity but you should be able to find some means to establish a starting point for each of these four factors. The second factor that some patients will be aware of is the ***frequency*** of the symptoms—daily, several times a day, a few times a week, etc. The next two, however, are seldom recognized by patients and these are what I refer to as ***stress capacity*** and ***rebound capacity***. If you have questioned your patient carefully during the intake, you will often find that their symptoms can be set-off by certain triggers. In the example I used of the hypothetical patient named Sara in Chapter Eleven, you learned that she could stand for 10-15 minutes and walk one block before her pain flared-up. This is the indication of her stress capacity. Standing and walking stress her problem and you made note of how much of that stress she could tolerate before her pain flared. You also learned that when the pain did flair, she would need to lie down for a few hours before it subsided again. This is an indication of her rebound capacity.

In those cases when you ask your patient how they are feeling since the time of their last treatment and they tell you that they are feeling "the same", with no noticeable improvement, you need to refer to your intake notes and what your patient told you about these four factors. They may have told you at first that their pain was an 8 on the 1-10 pain scale and are now telling you it is a 6. They may also have told you their symptoms were flaring everyday and now, when you question them in more detail, they indicate it is only happening about every other day. But even if their intensity and frequency are the same, you will often find there may have been improvement in either the stress or rebound capacity. This type of improvement may seem so insignificant to your patient that they don't notice it but here is the good news: If you can make and hold an improvement in any of these four factors, it is only a matter of time before the others start to show improvement too.

I tell my patients that since the treatment is sparking their internal resources, I cannot control which of these four factors will start to improve first but when any one of these show sustained improvement, the others will start to follow. Explaining this to your patients should encourage them to give the treatment a little more time and hopefully in that time the momentum will build and improvement in the intensity and frequency will follow. This can be crucial as some patients will be ready to stop the treatment without telling you if they have not perceived any benefit by the fifth or sixth treatment. If they actually did experience some benefit in the stress or rebound capacity, helping them to realize this can make the difference in them deciding to give it a few more treatments.

The final (plus one) factor you should ask about is medication levels. I keep referring to it as "(plus one)" because I don't advise my patients to change their medications in the beginning of a treatment process. Doing so complicates measuring the other four factors but some patients will take it upon themselves to reduce their medications without telling you even if you tell them not to. If they tell you they feel the same, ask about their medications because they may have reduced them. If you find out they are taking less of the medications that were reducing the symptoms you are measuring, this could well be an indication of improvement.

Just how you employ monitoring these four (plus one) factors can vary. You might want to inform each patient from the very beginning that you will be monitoring these. I don't usually do this because most of my patients have enough perceived benefit early enough that I don't have to worry about helping them see more subtle improvement. I only go over these factors when I reach the third or fourth treatment and the patient continues to tell me they are not noticing any improvement. Most of the time when I go over this with such a patient, the next time or two I see them, they will have noticed at least one of these factors has improved. That is important in that it usually means they are willing to give it at least another two or three more treatments. However, if the perceived benefit does not steadily grow in those two or three later treatments, I may very well be telling them how sorry I am that I was not able to help them and then look to advise them on any other resources they may want to try. You can't win them all.

Whether you advise your patient that you will be monitoring these factors at the time of their first treatment or wait until you sense they are getting frustrated with the lack of progress, you need to be ready to measure them by gathering the information on these factors during the initial intake. Don't assume that everyone will see marked benefit early enough that this detailed monitoring will not be needed. It is better to have this information and not need it than to need it and not have it.

Chapter Recap:

1. **The pressure to produce a perceived benefit within the first 5-6 treatments makes careful monitoring of progress important.**

2. The main areas to monitor are intensity, frequency, stress capacity, rebound capacity, and medication levels.

3. Maintaining improvement in any one of these factors will lead to improvement in all of them.

4. You can either tell your patients to watch for changes in these factors in the beginning of the treatment process or wait until you think they are concerned about lack of progress.

CHAPTER FOURTEEN

Self-Care

I mentioned in a previous chapter that I strive to get the most benefit out of as few treatments as possible and that a big part of doing this is educating patients about self-care. I cannot emphasize enough how important it can be to educate your patients about how their activities between treatments will affect the treatment outcome. Every day, a large percentage of acupuncture patients squander the benefits their treatments were beginning to provide by aggravating their condition and undermining their own healing. To better explain what I mean by this statement, I will use the example of treating musculoskeletal conditions as these tend to be a large part of many acupuncturists' practices and lend themselves well to the larger point I am trying to make. Understand, however, that my advice here is not just for those conditions. Anything that aggravates the condition you are trying to help should be watched for and avoided.

By understanding what I have been stressing from the beginning of this book—that acupuncture squeezes more out of the body's resources—you can understand why it can be so important that your patients are careful to avoid anything that aggravates their condition in the crucial beginning stage when you are trying to spark momentum. I mentioned earlier that I sometimes tell my patients that the beginning of the treatment is like planting seeds in a garden. We sow some seeds with the first treatments then wait for a sprout—the first signs of improvement in any of the four plus one factors. Once a seed germinates into a sprout, you have the potential for a future harvest but you must tend the sprout carefully because at this stage the sprout is weak and vulnerable. We still need to build momentum.

Many patients with musculoskeletal conditions have been encouraged to do exercises to try to "work out" the pain and stiffness. This often backfires and ends up aggravating these problems. I advise all my musculoskeletal patients that, while I want them to be as active as *safely* possible, I would rather they erred on the side of being underactive rather than overactive. I tell them that I am going to be monitoring their progress carefully and that since the beginning stage is so critical to the overall treatment process, I want them to avoid anything that has the chance of aggravating their problem. We must nurture the sprout, not stress it. This will often cause patients a lot of doubt and concern. They will worry that being inactive will make them worse or that they will lose their ability to be active. I address this by stressing that being extra careful this way is only a temporary precaution while we get the treatment process started. Once they are doing better—as the sprout sinks its roots in deeper—they can start to become more active again. I also point out that if their exercising had worked for them they wouldn't be coming to see someone like me. I ask them to give my advice of being extra careful 2-3 weeks to give these treatments the best chance of working.

When I start emphasizing this with my patients, they will ask questions about whether they can do this activity or not or this exercise or not. I tell them that it is impossible to tell different people just what activities will aggravate their condition. Some patients with low back pain, for example, will tell you that walking bothers their back while other patients that seem to have the same type of problem will tell you that walking makes it feel better. The way anyone can tell if the activity is likely aggravating their condition is to listen to what their body is telling them. Here is what I stress with my patients: ***Anything that makes the very problem we are trying to make go away act-up is probably bad for it. Anything that makes that problem feel comforted and relieved is probably good for it. Do more of the activities that make the problem feel relieved and less of those activities that make the problem act-up.***

I especially stress that I don't want my patients doing any exercises or anything else that causes more pain thinking it to be a matter of "No pain, no gain." That old adage is correct for increasing function in atrophied but intact tissues but ***not for injured, compromised tissues***. Pain is a sign of injury and you don't exercise your way out of an injury.

I tell my musculoskeletal patients to think of their problem like a sprained ankle. You don't exercise a sprained ankle in a no pain, no gain fashion as that would make it worse. You stay off of it until the pain goes down then gingerly try putting a little weight on it, testing if it is ready for more stress. If it starts to hurt, you know you just did too much too soon and you rest it again until it feels better and then you can try to put more weight on it again. That is exactly how to safely manage most conditions. Don't push it!

More Steps Forward - Less Steps Backwards

I stress that the whole strategy I am employing to get my patients the most benefit with the least number of treatments is one of taking more steps forward and less steps backward. The treatments will take the repair of their problem more steps forward by boosting their body's self-healing efforts by 10%-20%. If they will then do more of what relieves their problem and less of what makes it act-up, that will mean they are taking fewer steps backward. Momentum in the treatment process comes when we tip the body's struggle to the positive side. Taking more steps forward and less back will get us past this tipping point more quickly and with the least number of treatments.

As I mentioned, while it is easier to see this problem of steps backward taking place in musculoskeletal problems, the same issue happens in many other conditions. Patients with headaches should avoid eye strain and people with digestive issues should avoid irregular eating patterns or irritating foods. Poor sleeping habits will adversely affect all self-healing as the body does most of its repair work overnight so ask about your patients' sleep habits and work with them to improve those if they are a problem. Every little bit you can do to help the body to take more steps forward and that your patients can do to avoid taking even little steps backward will help. You only have five or six treatments to get a perceived benefit for your patients in most cases so you had better worry about even the smallest details!

In addition to imploring your patients to not aggravate the condition you are working so hard to help with the least cost possible, you should look to give them something they can do between treatments to take even more steps forward. Having your musculoskeletal patients regularly rub-in a good herbal liniment or use medicated plasters, for example, will help. Of course, if you use herbs in your practice, prescribing those is a big help. You can also teach your patients to do some self-acupressure or massage techniques. Other self-care methods include using a heating pad or ice or doing qi-gong or tai chi or teaching breathing or meditative practices.

Give your patients something that they can do themselves so that they will be more active in their care. This will improve the odds of success more so than if you just do your treatments on them and your patients only responsibility is to show up for the treatment. Make sure what you give them to do at home is as safe as possible. It is also useful to give them handouts explaining the self-care methods with any precautions clearly spelled out.

I hope you will heed my warning about how patients often reduce the effectiveness of your treatments by what they do to themselves once they walk out your door. Once I began to emphasize this in my practice, my success rates went up. This same warning also applies for therapies you may employ like acupressure or tui-na. There is a fine line between under-doing and overdoing. It is wisest to err on the side of under-doing. That is why the great Greek physician Hippocrates warned to "First, do no harm." As healers we cannot always know we are doing the right thing for our patients but we should at least make sure we are not making them worse. It is difficult to harm people with acupuncture because it is such a modest manipulation of the body. Once you start doing hands-on therapies, the risk of causing harm goes up.

Chapter Recap:

1. **Early stages of progress can be fragile and easily lost if patients overstress themselves.**

2. **Many patients will worry about being inactive but you should stress being extra careful is only temporary in the beginning stage of treatment.**

3. **Advise your patients that anything that makes the problem you are treating more noticeable is bad for it while anything that makes that problem feel relieved is good for it.**

4. **Strive to help your patients take more steps forward and fewer steps backward.**

5. **Give you patients something to do themselves between visits such as taking herbs, using liniments and/or plasters, or doing self-massage/acupressure.**

CHAPTER FIFTEEN

The Treatment Process

OK. You conducted a complimentary consultation and your prospective patient has agreed to become an actual patient after you estimated the odds of success, how many treatments it should take to see the first signs of progress, explained the treatment process as taking part in three stages, and emphasized that you will keep them informed as to how they seem to be responding to the first series of treatments. Now the pressure is on to deliver a perceived benefit at a manageable cost in a pleasant environment within that initial series of treatments and establish momentum with as few treatments as possible. As I mentioned in the introduction, I am not going to be trying to teach specific methods of diagnosis and treatment for specific conditions although I will offer some of my favorite point combinations for common conditions near the end of this book. Whatever methods you use to determine what points and techniques you employ for whatever conditions you are treating, the following advice should increase your success rates and especially improve the rates of patient satisfaction.

I have already detailed my advice on how to space the treatments in the beginning stages. You want to treat at twice a week for the first two to three weeks or at very least, three treatments in the first 7-9 days. You have taken a history that details the patient's current pattern of symptoms, especially noting how the symptoms vary in intensity, frequency, stress capacity, and rebound capacity as well as the medications they are taking for those symptoms. This history gives you baseline measurements you will measure progress against during the treatment process.

When I begin a treatment, I try to keep my patients as covered as possible while still exposing the skin needed to do any examination and treatment I wish to do. I advise my patients to wear loose fitting clothes for the treatment so they can leave on as much of their clothing as possible. What I find works best for me is using clean towels instead of gowns. Using towels allows more flexibility in exposing skin while keeping other areas covered. Once I determine what points I will be using and so what position I want the patient in, I will explain this to them, have the towel(s) ready for them, and then leave the room with the door closed while they get ready. I let them know I will be stepping out to wash my hands and be back for them in a moment.

Once enough time has passed for them to have gotten ready, I knock on the door and ask if they are ready, waiting to hear that they are before entering. I use the paper towel I dried my hands with after washing them to open the door (so as not to touch the door handle with my clean hands) and then lay that paper towel on my shelf as a little clean area near my needles. You want to make sure your patient will be comfortable throughout the treatment. This is not only a nice thing to do for them but helps to make the treatment more effective. Being that the treatment will be stimulating the patient's internal resources, the more relaxed the patient is, the easier it will be for those resources to be stimulated. I try to have the treatment environment set-up that will allow the patient to fall asleep or at least slip into the beautiful not awake yet not asleep state acupuncture so often causes. I make sure I ask them if they are comfortable before proceeding with the treatment and will make any adjustments necessary to make this the case.

After I have inserted the needles I let the patient know that they don't have to remain perfectly still just because they have needles in them. Some patients worry so much about this that it causes them stress because they are afraid to move even in the slightest. I tell my patients they are free to move a bit if they need to in order to stay comfortable and while this may cause a slight pinching at some points this should fade within 30-60 seconds once they stop moving again. I let them know that if I ever need them to not move part of their body because of a needle, I will make this clear. Otherwise shifting a bit to stay comfortable is fine. In my old office, I told my patients to call out if anything bothers them because I would be close enough to the treatment rooms I could hear them easily. Some practitioners will use some sort of signaling system in their treatment rooms that patients can use if they need attention. One of the better such devices is a wireless doorbell. Others may just have a little bell the patient can ring. In my newest, larger office, we set up a system of baby monitors that I switch on before I leave the room for those patients that might have difficulty calling out. However you manage this, let your patients know they don't have to stay as still as a statue during the treatment and give them a means to alert you if they need attention as this will reduce their stress.

When enough time has passed with the needles in, I knock lightly on the door and wait a second before entering. Many patients will have fallen asleep or be in a state of deep relaxation during the treatment and if you enter the treatment room without some sort of noise first, they may become startled by your presence—kind of like being asleep in your bed and suddenly realizing a stranger is standing over you. Announcing yourself before entering the treatment room gives the patient a chance to snap out of the deep relaxation state acupuncture so often causes and not be startled.

Once I take the needles out, I will do some acupressure/massage work on my patients. I really encourage you to do this as it helps to finish the treatment in a positive way—like icing on the cake. This is most useful when treating muscular problems but even in other cases a few minutes of a nice back rub is welcomed by virtually all patients. At very least you should rub the spots where the needles were inserted for a second or two even if you are doing a *qi* venting technique (just wait a few seconds before rubbing). Inserting even a hair-fine acupuncture needle, while ultimately a good thing for the body, is still a shock and insult to the affected tissues. Giving those tissues a little gentle rub after the needle is removed helps smooth this insult and leaves the body feeling better about the whole process. It is during the time I am doing the acupressure/massage that I give my patients any advice I have for self-care or what they should do between the treatments as I explained in the previous chapter.

Follow-Up Treatments

When the patient returns for their next appointment, I will ask them how they have been feeling since I saw them last. If they tell me they have been feeling much better since then, that means we have gotten over the first and most important hurdle of getting that first sprout of progress and we are now into the middle stage of trying to hold and build on that improvement. I will emphasize that is it very important for them to not get overconfident and think they can start to do those things that would set their condition off in the past. The roots of the sprout are not deep enough yet for them to do those types of things. They need to continue to be careful until more time has passed and we have built on their initial progress. It is vital to emphasize this as many patients will be so happy to finally be feeling better they will want to make up for lost time and run the risk of erasing the progress before it is stable enough to take the stress.

If during this next appointment, however, the patient tells me they are feeling the same, I will ask them about each of the four factors of intensity, frequency, stress capacity, and rebound capacity I detailed in Chapter Thirteen. I am careful just how I do this. I don't want to grill them or seem like I doubt what they are telling me. I just want to make sure there really has been no progress. I will let them know it often takes a few treatments before that first sprout of progress appears but to please pay attention to each of the four factors and let me know if there are any changes when I see them next. If there is truly no improvement after the first few treatments, I will change the treatment approach (switch to plan B), but, if there is even modest improvement in any of the four factors, I will want to stay with the original approach as greater progress should soon follow.

Releasing Patients and Maintenance Care

In Chapter Twelve, I offered advice on how to space treatments in order to spark and ride momentum to achieve maximum therapeutic benefit with the least number of treatments. Once you have gotten the maximum benefit out of the treatment process it is time to release patients from your care. If you were treating an acute condition, there is no need for the patient to come back for any maintenance. If you were treating a chronic condition, however, it is often helpful to do some regular maintenance treatment to help reduce the chance the problem will return.

I do not routinely advise my patients to keep seeing me for maintenance care unless they ask about it and seem open to it. While I think everyone can benefit from regular acupuncture, the reason I don't recommend this to all my patients is that I don't want them to think that once they come to me for one problem, I will be telling them they should keep coming back for treatments for the rest of their lives. I think doing this runs the risk of losing credibility with some people but that is just my take on the issue. What I tell my patients is to let me know if their symptoms return for more than 3-4 days. They may have a little flair-up for a day or two but if things then settle back down there is nothing that needs to be done. Any symptoms lasting more than 3-4 days should be treated quickly and not allowed to go on for weeks as doing so will then require more treatments to bring things back under control.

All of the advice I have offered for the entire treatment process is based on trying to squeeze the most benefit from the least number of treatments and with a low average out-of-pocket expense. Managing your practice in this way will give you the best chance of building a stable practice. You will occasionally have some patients who are not so concerned about keeping the cost of treatment to its lowest and will be open to doing treatments more frequently and in doing routine maintenance. Such patients make your job easier and are wonderful to have. Your chances of having such patients decide to do this are actually higher if you follow the protocols for getting the most from the least. When your patients see that you are trying your best to keep costs down, those who can afford to do more will have more trust in you and will be more likely to work with you in that manner.

Managing Patients with Multiple Problems

Finally, I wanted to touch on how to prioritize treatment in patients with multiple problems. This can be a great challenge especially in getting a patient's treatment off to the best start possible. A patient comes to you with a stubborn problem like ten years of back pain that has not been helped by months of physical therapy, years of drugs, and perhaps dozens of chiropractic treatments. They then balk when you suggest it may take 8-10 treatments with acupuncture but hesitantly agree to give the first 5 or 6 treatments a try. They then ask if you could also help them for their carpal tunnel, planter fasciitis, acid reflux, and depression. Considering it took your best effort to get them to agree to the initial 5-6 treatments for the low back problem, you can bet they are not ready to give an additional 5-6 treatments for each of these other problems.

What I tell my patients in these situations is that while it is certainly possible to treat more than one problem at a time with acupuncture, just how we spread the focus of the treatment is important in the beginning stages. Because the treatment stimulates the body's internal resources and there is a limit to those resources, trying to treat too many problems at once will spread those resources so thin, it will tend to take longer to help anything. Since most people will not keep coming for treatment if they don't see progress in the beginning stages, one needs to be careful how he/she prioritizes the treatment. I ask these types of patients to list for me their top three problems in order of priority. Which is the most important problem they want help for then which is number two and number three?

Once I have an understanding of the patients top priorities, I can evaluate how I believe they would respond to treatment. What you hope for is that the top priorities are also the ones that should respond most readily to the treatment although that seldom happens. You don't want to waste too much effort on trying to help a lower priority problem that is also going to be very stubborn and take a lot of time and effort to get improvement for. You do, however, need to do everything you can to help the number one priority no matter how difficult it may be to treat.

Again, you can get a sense about just how readily different problems should respond to treatment by using my method of estimating the odds of success based on the variability of the pattern of symptoms and the others factors I detailed for you in Chapter Nine. In some cases, I will tell my patient that we need to concentrate on the number one problem first and then we can add numbers two and three once we get the ball rolling on number one. Or, I might tell them I will focus about 70% of the treatment on number one and 30% on number two and once number one is doing better, we can begin to shift that focus to 50%-50% and then perhaps 30%-70%. At some point, if things are going well, we can add the number three problem into the mix. Yet another scenario may be when a patient's number one problem is one that figures to take a longer time to expect improvement while the number three problem has a good chance of responding soon. In these cases you might want to split the treatment about 50%-50% between the two trying to get some improvement for the number three problem early on while starting the longer process of beginning to help problem number one. If the patient sees improvement in problem number three, they will probably be happy enough about that to give the treatment enough time to get the ball rolling on problem number one.

I don't know how many of you reading this may be familiar with the old-fashioned entertainment acts that used to be popular in the U.S. from Vaudeville days up until the late 1960's that involved spinning many dish plates at once on thin poles. The entertainer would get one plate started spinning, and then another, then another but would have to watch for any plate that began wobbling and rush back to give that plate a spin to keep it going. That is similar to what can happen treating several problems at once with acupuncture. You get the first ones going and then add for more checking all the while to make sure you are not losing progress and giving those ones an extra focus if they start to wobble.

Managing patients with multiple problems under the market pressures of cost and time is one of the most difficult problems we face in private practice and I hope the advice above is at least some help to you in this. There is no simple formula for how to prioritize these cases. Learning to do so takes time. As many of these cases would benefit from many treatments over a longer period of time, these patients might be better off being treated in a Community Acupuncture setting with the availability of very low fees. If you live in an area with an A/OM college, these may also have low fees in their intern clinics. Such clinics can be a good choice for some patients with difficult cases because they will often have experienced practitioners working with multiple interns discussing such cases in great detail. You don't need to try to treat everyone yourself. If you see a patient that wants treatment for multiple problems and cannot afford what it would likely take under your pricing structure and there are lower-cost resources available, go ahead and refer out to them. Or, if your patient load is low and you have the time, give a good discount to help these patients be able to afford the number of treatments they need. Just do everything you can to help your patients even if that means referring them to a competitor. Putting the patient's well being first will always benefit you in the long run.

Chapter Recap:

1. Try to make your patients as comfortable as possible during the treatment.

2. Clean towels can help to keep patients as covered as possible while exposing the skin needed for treatment.

3. If washing hands outside the treatment room, the paper towel you used to dry your hands can be used to open the door handle to keep hands clean.

4. After inserting the needles, let the patient know they do not have to remain perfectly still and have a means that allows them to alert you if they need attention.

5. Knock on the door before entering and reentering the room.

6. Do some acupressure massage at the end of the treatment while advising patients on self-care instructions.

7. Monitor progress with each follow-up treatment and release from care when maximum therapeutic benefit is reached.

8. Offer maintenance care if the patient expresses an interest in it but don't advise this for every patient.

9. For patients with multiple problems, have them prioritize the most important three then try to balance their treatment with those priorities in mind.

CHAPTER SIXTEEN

More on Fees and Money

In the chapter on establishing your fees, I offered my thoughts on the subject of fees for acupuncture in general and about my current fee structure. In this chapter, I want to offer some more perspective on how I manage my fees including how accepting insurance can play a role in setting fees. I will give more information on insurance in the following chapter and then we will consider some of the details of how to open an office and get those first patients in your door.

I mentioned earlier that I charge different rates for children, adults, and elderly patients and that such a policy should be acceptable even in states that may have regulations against such practices as it reflects different amounts of patient contact time. Again, you should research just how you need to establish this policy if your state has such ridiculous regulations because being able to charge different rates has significant advantages in keeping your patients' average out-of-pocket expenses low. Because my model encourages accepting insurance, those patients with insurance coverage often end up paying the least out-of-pocket. As Social Security does not cover acupuncture, few elderly patients will have insurance coverage and so it is important that their fees be lower than younger adults. Again, this can be justified by the fact that you should not have to leave the needles in quite as long in elderly patients and that some elderly patients will not be comfortable for as long a period of time during the treatment. Children will also tend to have little or no insurance coverage but they can also be adequately treated in less time than adults.

Of course, not all non-senior adults will have insurance coverage but, as compared to the other age groups, even those without insurance will generally be in a better position to manage your "usual" fees. No single fee structure will work in all circumstances for both the patients' best interest as well as struggling practitioners but the model I have described strikes what I believe to be the best balance at this time. Having this flexibility in fees will help on many levels.

One advantage to having different set fees for different age groups/time spent is it allows you to explain to those who qualify for those lower fees that you are making allowances for them. When I explain my fees to a geriatric patient or the parents of a pediatric patient I always start by letting them know my usual fees are $60 but I only charge $40 or $30 or whatever the case may be for their age group/situation. This is important for two reasons: First, it suggests they are getting a price break and that is always welcomed news to a new patient. Second, it alerts patients that these lower prices are just for certain age groups. You want your patients to know those details so they won't refer a patient to you who thinks they will get the same price if he/she doesn't qualify.

One of the tricky aspects of setting your fees is factoring-in how accepting insurance will influence those fees. In my practice model, insurance is accepted as I strive to make my services available to the widest possible range of potential patients and keep the out of pocket expense to a low average. I am going to advise you on insurance in the next section but mention it here because the decision to accept insurance or not should be part of what you consider setting your fees. Why? You don't want to have two sets of fees; one for cash patients and then another for insurance patients. Doing so leaves you open to insurance fraud. Yet, you would like to take advantage of the few insurance plans out there that pay for acupuncture at a higher rate than is feasible to charge cash patients in many markets.

Let's assume you decide to accept insurance as my model encourages but you realize there is a problem we face in this profession that seems unfair. In the U.S., our system is geared to have most medical service fees paid for out of a third party payor system (insurance). If you are a medical service provider that has little or no coverage within the third party system, you are at a double disadvantage. Your patients have to pay out of pocket for your services but they don't have as much money in their pocket since some of it was siphoned-off to pay into the third-party system. The trouble we have in our field then is we need to make our treatments affordable to the large percentage of cash patients we rely on and yet take advantage of the limited insurance coverage when it is available. Unfortunately, as I said, you can't legally charge higher for insurance than you do for cash. If most of our patients were covered by insurance at say, $100 a treatment, you could charge $100 a treatment and let those few who don't have insurance worry about how to pay for it. Since that is not the case, acupuncturists need those cash patients as the foundation of their practices while trying to take advantage of any insurance that will pay more than your market's cash rates while not having a dual price system.

One way you can approach this catch-22 that is in the grey area of legality—not clearly illegal and maybe perfectly legal—is by charging for different services. Say you charge $50 for acupuncture but when you bill insurance you also add your charges for acupressure/massage or the heat lamp therapy you did. This might bring your charges up to $90-$100 for example. Some insurance companies will pay on some of those additional services, others will not. But as long as you provided those services, it is perfectly legal to charge for them. It should be up to you, however, to decide whether or not you charge any specific patient for those additional services. While I am not an attorney, I can't imagine that it is illegal to provide a service to a patient and decide to not charge them for it. So as long as you have a single charge for acupuncture that you stick to for both insurance and cash patients, you should be able to decide whether or not you charge any individual patient for additional services you provided. You should not have a policy that says you always do acupressure/massage and heat therapy every time you do acupuncture and you always charge insurance companies for those additional services but never charge cash patients for them, but you should have the legal ability to decide if you want to provide an additional service and not charge for it. Again, I am not an attorney and I am not advising you about the legality of this strategy. You need to check local laws and decide for yourself how you set your policies. I am just stating my opinion about what seems reasonable. I will tell you this: Never bill an insurance company for any service you did not provide. Don't do it. It is not worth it and is clearly illegal.

The next wrinkle you should consider when setting your fees while also accepting insurance is the prevalence of "discount" insurance programs also sometimes referred to as "access" programs. These programs often complement HMO plans or may replace HMO plans. These plans are not "benefit" plans, meaning those that have a set fee schedule and would require you to follow specific guidelines for what conditions can be treated, what you will be paid, and how many treatments you can do. I will explain more about these different plans in the next chapter. The reason I bring up discount plans in this section on setting fees is that if you sign-on with a network that offers discount plans, you are agreeing to offer a discount off your normal fees – usually around 25%. The good thing about patients with discount plans is that, unlike the benefit plans, there is (usually) no paperwork, and you can treat any condition and as often as you want without getting any approval. These patients are essentially cash patients but given a discount. The bad thing is you agree to give a 25% discount and if your fees are already low to help make them affordable, that 25% discount can push your fee to below what seems reasonable. For this reason, my advice is you set your fees for acupuncture at just a little above what you calculate as the lowest you should charge trying to strike that delicate balance between affordability and what is reasonable for your time. In my example, I would be fine with getting $40 - $50 a treatment but I charge $60 for non-seniors/children so I have a little wiggle-room for the discount programs and for those insurance plans that would pay at $60 or more.

The last thought I want to share with you on this subject of setting fees and avoiding a two-tiered pricing policy for insurance and cash is that there is some legal grounds for charging slightly less for cash. Again, I am not an attorney nor am I giving legal advice but I have read some opinions that a modest "discount for cash" policy has been argued as legal but I don't know if this would be a state by state issue or if this has been settled.

Reducing Cash Payment Fatigue

One of the more important tricks of the trade I learned after four or five years of practice is how to reduce what could be called "cash payment fatigue." This refers to what happens when a cash patient has been paying for their treatments and they get to a point when they begin to wonder how much longer they will be reaching into their wallet—how many more treatments they will need before they are finally finished. I found that many patients start to get payment fatigue around the eighth treatment or so. I am referring here to a patient that is improving and is generally happy with their progress but the costs are starting to add-up and the patient starts worrying about how much longer this will go on.

What I began to do to limit this and still have as a policy 20 years later, is to give a $10 discount after the eighth treatment. I only do this for those I was charging $60 a treatment, reducing it to $50. I don't offer this to my geriatric or pediatric patients because I am already charging them less than my full fee. You would be surprised at just how grateful patients are for this modest discount. I have seen this happen hundreds of times and patients will be so grateful that they will often be comfortable continuing for several more treatments than they would have if I had kept charging the same rate. A patient may decide that they just can't keep justifying the cost and stop after 12 treatments, for example, when, if you would have reduced the fee by $10 beginning on the 9th treatment, they may have keep coming to you for 15-16 treatments and received the full benefit of your treatments.

You can try using this policy in two basic ways and figure out for yourself which way works best. One way is that you can mention this discount when you are first explaining your charges during an initial consultation. The advantage to this is that it helps you to educate your patients about how many treatments may be needed. You let them know you have a policy that gives them a discount if they need to keep coming for more than 8 treatments. You tell them that most cases you treat should be done by 6-8 treatments so you give this discount to help make the charges more affordable for those more difficult cases. This really helps as many of your chronic condition patients will need to keep coming more than 8 times. Explaining this discount lets them know that if they need more than 8 treatments it is because they are more difficult to treat. Many people will recognize that they are a very difficult case and they will be grateful that you are reducing your fees to help accommodate them.

Do you see the beauty of this approach? You are letting the patient know that most people are not so difficult to treat and that if they need more than 8 treatments, it means they are a difficult case. It suggests that the higher costs of higher treatment numbers is not the fault of the treatment itself or your services, it is their fault for being such a difficult case. On top of that, it makes you out to be the one who is being generous by giving them a break. You are not only taking on a difficult case that will require more work on your part than normal, but you are going to give them a discount as well.

I don't mean to sound crass by putting it as I have above and I don't see this policy as manipulating a patient. I started giving this discount when I sensed some of my patients were worrying about the ongoing treatment costs and I just wanted to give them a break. It was only afterward that I found that patients tended to keep coming for more treatments and that this was such a useful tool to help educate patients about the realities of treating chronic conditions. People of course hope they could have a few treatments and a 30 year problem will go away but they do understand when you let them know that acupuncture can manage some conditions quickly but others require more prolonged therapy. Explaining your discount policy allows you to do this in a way that softens the blow of learning they will likely need more extended treatment and puts a positive spin on this reality.

The second way you can inform a patient about this discount is to just wait until you get to the eighth treatment and spring it on them. You might do this if you sense the patient does not seem too worried about needing more than 8 treatments when you do your initial consultation. If they seem OK with continuing treatment past the eighth one, offering this discount will be a welcome bonus. Maybe they would have been fine with continuing with the full price but the discount will make you seem even more helpful in their eyes and improve the level of patient satisfaction. Besides, you might have read them wrong. Maybe they seemed to be fine continuing at full price but they may have just been better at masking their payment fatigue and might have stopped coming for treatment before you were finished without saying a word.

As a general rule, I don't have employees in my front office mention the discount when someone calls or walks in our office asking about our services and prices. I don't tell them to not mention this and if they sense it will make a positive difference I leave that up to them, but I would usually rather leave that up to me to use as a means of facilitating the best relationship with my patients.

CHAPTER SEVENTEEN

Accepting Insurance

Just as there are plenty of resources out there teaching about diagnosis and treatment, there are also resources for learning about how to bill insurance for coverage of your services. I am not going to try to cover this whole topic and encourage you to get as much training on this subject as you can. My practice model relies on accepting insurance because when you are trying to build a private practice, it is in your best interest to do everything within reason to not limit the types of patients you accept and to keep their out-of-pocket costs to a minimum. You also need to learn as much as you can in these first years about every facet of running a practice so you can better manage your career moving forward. I have found that some in the A/OM profession have misunderstandings regarding insurance and I would like to offer some advice here you might not get elsewhere. I already offered some of this information in the section on setting your fees. Please read that section to get that information also.

The question of whether or not to accept insurance is a hot topic among some acupuncturists. Those that are opposed to accepting insurance fall into two general categories; those who just don't want to be bothered with all the red tape or low fees and those who oppose the influence accepting insurance can have on the delivery of care. Some see accepting insurance as a slippery slope that can corrupt practitioners and bankrupt healing professions. I can't say that those who feel that way are wrong as I agree there are negatives associated with relying on third party payment to any large degree. I just don't tend to see this as having a greater negative than positive for the A/OM profession at this stage for many reasons. Even though I don't necessarily agree with those who fear the influence of insurance on the A/OM profession, I actually respect those who don't accept insurance based on those types of principals. They might be right and I might be wrong in the long-run but I continue to feel that accepting insurance is important for those just starting out to have the best chance to survive in private practice.

I also respect those who don't accept insurance because of the trouble of dealing with all the paperwork—if these practitioners are earning all they wish to earn. I have little sympathy for those who are struggling financially in their practice and don't want to accept insurance because of the paperwork. Surviving in practice takes a smart, continuous effort as you attempt to build a steady flow of patients. You really need to give yourself every opportunity to build your patient base and turning away potential patients because you don't want to deal with some paperwork is plain foolish—and lazy.

Is insurance red tape a pain in the butt? Sure. But you are trying to build a successful business as a small, self-employed entrepreneur. To survive as an acupuncturist you must become an effective problem solver. Learning how to manage insurance is just one of the many problems you need to manage, especially considering it is one that helps you get paid. You want to make it as easy as possible for as many people as possible to make use of your services, so why would you turn away business unless you were either too busy or too rich or if you have a strong ethical aversion to working with insurance corporations? There are many unexciting tasks in which you will need to become proficient like maintaining patient charts, accounting, dealing with leases, advertising/marketing, etc. Insurance is just one more in a long list of these so don't be a crybaby about it; look at it as just one more skill you need to build in your quest to achieve the blessing of earning a comfortable living while helping others and move on.

The last thought I want to mention on this subject of the hassle of insurance paperwork is that it really only becomes a significant issue when you are seeing a lot of insurance patients. If your patient load is modest, you have lots of time to deal with paperwork. Once you get to the point of having many insurance patients and the paperwork really does present problems, you can decide then how to deal with it. You might be in a strong enough position at that time to stop accepting insurance and just give your patients statements they can turn-in to their insurance companies after paying you at the time of service, or you may find it best to hire a billing service. Or do what I ended-up doing and have your spouse manage insurance billing. Whatever you decide, don't worry about it until you have lots of insurance patients. At that point, it is a pretty nice problem to have.

Under the broad heading of "insurance", there are several different types: There is the rapidly declining so-called "fee for service" (indemnity) plans, managed care plans, workers compensation-type plans, and personal injury cases that might be covered under insurance or might be done under a lien. As of the time of my writing this, Medicare does not cover acupuncture although there is an effort to pass legislation that will do so. There is also great debate about health care or health insurance reform going on in our government although it seems unlikely a "new" type of insurance plan will come-out of this. I suggest you get familiar with all these types so you can make informed decisions about whether or not you work with any or all of them. I have worked with all these types of insurance over the years but what I want to go into some detail on here is managed care plans. I have the most experience with this type of plan and this is the most rapidly growing type of insurance and may be the type under which acupuncture is most covered.

Managed Care Insurance Plans

In using the term **managed care**, I am referring to a system in which a provider of services signs a contractual agreement with an insurance company and agrees to specific terms. While the terms for payment of services can vary under these systems (see below), the common features include the provider signing a contract and having their credentials checked before being accepted (credentialed) into a **network** of providers. Part of the credentialing process may involve attesting to certain questions and will include providing proof of malpractice insurance.

Access and Benefit Plans

There are two basic types of managed care plans currently being utilized for complementary and alternative medicine (CAM) services: **Access plans** and **Benefit plans**. Benefit plans provide specific benefits to members (patients), including the number of treatments allowed per year, which medical conditions are covered under the plan, co-payments, deductibles, and so forth. Some of these plans are purchased as rider plans similar to purchasing dental or vision coverage and require the service provider to obtain approval for most if not all of the treatments they wish to perform.

Benefit plans require providers to bill the insurance company for their services and not bill the patient any additional fees other than co-payments or deductibles. Providers are then paid by the insurance company based on a set **fee schedule**.

Access plans are also called **discount plans** because providers offer a discount off of their normal fees (usually between 20-25%). These plans are offered by insurance companies to their members at no cost. Members are encouraged to go to their insurance company's network of credentialed providers to obtain the discount. Eligible members can be treated for any condition, require no authorization for treatment, and pay out of pocket for their treatment. Access plans are not money makers for insurance companies and are usually used to test the interest in a new market or as a form of token coverage.

Paperwork

Access plans require very little additional paperwork over what you already utilize. Some may ask providers to give patients some sort of satisfaction survey to be mailed back to the insurance company; some plans may want providers to have patients sign an informed consent form. One company I know of used to ask providers to fill out a receipt form for each patient that indicates the diagnosis and discount given but I am not sure if they are still doing this.

Benefit plans require providers to submit forms in order to obtain treatment authorization. Different companies will have somewhat different requirements in this regard. Most will encourage providers to fax these forms or use online submissions as soon as possible so they can be put through the case management review process. In this process, the patient's benefit status will first be verified. A utilization (case) manager will review the information submitted by the provider and decide whether to allow the treatments requested. The provider will then be sent some sort of authorization response informing them whether their proposed treatment plan has been accepted as requested, accepted with modifications, or denied.

The authorization process is a source of frustration for many providers, especially those not in the habit of filling out medical history/diagnosis forms. Waiting to be informed if your proposed treatments have been authorized is not something most acupuncturists are accustomed to, except perhaps in the treatment of workers' compensation cases. When deciding which managed care networks you will contract with, you may wish to inquire about their turnaround time for treatment authorizations, appeals processes for disputed authorizations, and the qualifications and training of their case managers. The better companies will be happy to provide you with this information. Or you may want to enroll in as many as you can and then decide which to stay with over time.

While some networks' paperwork procedures for treatment authorizations can be time-consuming, don't get too discouraged about the time it takes you to complete these forms in the beginning. With experience, you will reduce the time this process takes, just as most acupuncturists eventually learn how to reduce the time it takes to treat each patient.

Take the time to go over the information your network company has provided on completing their forms, then practice by filling out some forms before you see your first managed care patient. If you have any front office staff, have them familiarize themselves with the forms they will ask your patients to fill out. Finally, contact your network company if you have any questions regarding paperwork procedures. They should have representatives available to answer your questions in a timely manner.

Putting Reimbursement Rates Into Perspective:

Like most acupuncturists involved with managed care plans, I wish they paid more. While rates will vary somewhat, the company that has the most business in this market is American Specialty Health Networks (American Specialty Health Plans in California). The current rate they pay acupuncturists for most of their plans is $40. While many are upset with this rate, there are some important things to consider that often go overlooked.

What you should do when thinking about these rates is don't think of them as the most you will get for your treatments, think of them as the *least* you will get. The reason I say this is because most all of these plans will have specific limits on what they cover as part of their benefit. There will be limits on what is called "covered conditions" and "covered services."

The term "covered conditions" refers to just which types of medical conditions are included under the benefit and which are not. Most of these plans will pay for conditions involving pain but even those may be limited to specific musculo-skeletal conditions. The fact that acupuncturists can treat such a wide variety of conditions and these benefit plans are limited in the types of medical conditions they cover can be both a bad and a good thing. Say, for example, a patient comes to you for the treatment of a covered condition such as neck pain but also mention they want to quit smoking. You state you do treatment for quitting smoking but this is not a covered condition under their benefit plan. The patient decides to come to you for quit smoking and you have them sign a form that states the patient realize he/she will have to pay out-of-pocket for this treatment because it is not a covered condition. You are then free to treat that patient as a cash patient for however much you usually charge. It may be that you will average better than $40 per treatment when you factor in the cash fees you get for treating conditions that are not covered.

The same applies for non-covered services. Some of these plans will have specific language in the contracts that state that certain services are "non-covered." These may be services like acupressure/Oriental massage or cupping. If you believe your patient needs these services, you can discuss this with them and have them sign an agreement acknowledging that these are non-covered services and they are agreeing to pay for these out of pocket.

Even if a managed care patient does not end-up having treatment for non-covered conditions or non-covered services, if they are happy with your services, they may end-up referring several other patients who pay your going rates or have insurance that pays at a higher rate than the managed care plans do. This is what I mean by looking at the modest managed care rates as the least you will ever get. Building a practice is all about building a patient base and anything that brings in more patients helps you toward that goal. Don't get hung up on the short-term price points of these managed care rates, look at them as just one part of a multi-part strategy to build a patient base.

What tends to happen with managed care plans is that the number of patients you might have referred to you can vary dramatically. As I mentioned above, many of these plans are sold as rider plans, i.e., additional coverage on top of the basic medical. This type of rider is usually purchased by individual employer groups and not available to individuals to purchase. The reason such plans are usually not available for individual policyholders to purchase is that if someone buys one of these plans they will almost certainly use it and end up costing the insurance company more than they take-in for the additional policy. In a group plan, the employer is buying this additional coverage for many employees and the insurance company sets their fees based on calculations that only a percentage of all those who have the coverage will actually use it.

Because these plans are bought by employers, how many patients you may see from being in this type of network will depend on the number of employees in your area that have this insurance added to their basic medical plan. If a large employer in your area decides to add this type of rider plan, you may see a lot of referrals. If there are no employers offering this in your area, you likely won't see many at all although you may still get some that have the discount plans as far more group plans offer these due to their low cost.

CHAPTER EIGHTEEN

Office Location

Beyond any doubt, the most important factor that will shape how you go about establishing your practice is location and most especially, the city/town you settle in. While I firmly believe the potential for acupuncturists is unlimited because virtually everyone can benefit from acupuncture treatment, until we are successful in convincing the public that this is the case, acupuncturists trying to establish their practices had better be concerned about competition. Too many acupuncturists try to open practices in areas that already have large numbers of acupuncturists instead of locating in areas with few if any. Often, this happens when the newly licensed try to open practices in the cities they went to school in. As I mentioned above, this should not be a problem because only a fraction of the public who could be helped with this therapy are making use of it even in areas with high concentrations of acupuncturists. In reality, however, because people don't yet understand just how valuable acupuncture can be for them, practitioners starting out in cities with lots of competition face additional obstacles establishing their practices compared to those starting out in areas with little or no competition. While I will offer advice on how to establish your practice in areas with lots of competition, I want to spend some time discussing the benefits of establishing your practice in areas with little competition as doing so usually makes the task of building a practice much easier.

One factor that many may not appreciate is how well an acupuncture practice can be accepted in more conservative areas. I mentioned in the "My Story" section that I had opened my practice in a city on the eastern border of Los Angeles County that was quite conservative (at least by Los Angeles standards). In California, the vast majority of acupuncture schools are located along the coast and most acupuncture practices in California are clustered in coastal areas, especially near these schools. The farther inland you go, the fewer acupuncturists you will find. A good portion of the patient base in the areas closer to the coast consists of people with relatively higher incomes and college educations. Although stereotyping groups of people tends to oversimplify matters, I still think it's fair to say that a higher portion of acupuncture patients in these areas are progressive types already interested in holistic health and well-being. I saw very few of these types of patients in my first office. Most of the patients I treated then were of modest incomes and were not coming to me to get their chakras balanced. They had health problems that were so problematic they were doing something they never thought they would do; going to an acupuncturist (and one just out of school at that).

What I learned from treating this type of patient is that while they tended to be skeptical about what the treatments could do for them, once I was able to help them, they were extremely grateful and loyal. Win the skeptics over with good results at a reasonable cost and they will be loyal, long time patients who will be happy to refer others to you. I now have some patients who still come to me after more than 20 years. Being that my office was not all that far from the New Age leaning coastal areas, I would occasionally get a patient coming to me who had moved from those areas to where my office was located. They would tell me how happy they were to find someone like me in this area as they badly missed these types of resources that were so plentiful near the coast. They would also tell me how much they loved acupuncture and how they would be my best patient because they really understood how great Chinese medicine was. Much to my surprise, I found most of those types of patients to not be reliable at all. Maybe I didn't cater to them in the right way, but what I really came to believe was that they weren't so much looking for help with specific problems but were just trying out the latest New Age health fad. Again, stereotypes may be unfair but the point I want to raise here is that you don't need to look for areas where people are already accepting of Eastern or otherwise New Age practices to find a willing patient base and the stereotype that the more conservative aren't enlightened enough to understand acupuncture is not accurate. People understand effective results and those that are suffering don't really care about why things work or if their therapy reflects their life philosophy. They just want help and will be appreciative to anyone that can help them especially when others have failed.

The two states with the highest number of acupuncturists per capita are Hawaii and New Mexico, respectively. Trying to open a practice in Honolulu or Santa Fe would be difficult for most new practitioners and so might this prove true in places like Santa Monica, California or Seattle, Washington. When I speak of what town to open your practice in and understanding your competition, this can be approached in two ways: You can look to settle in a state that has few practitioners or you can also look in states with higher numbers of practitioners but that also have underserved towns. I live in California—the state that has the greatest number of acupuncturists and is third in the nation in acupuncturists per capita, but even in California, there are dozens of towns that don't have a single acupuncturist because of the way practitioners are clustered. Even when there is an acupuncturist in the town right next door, being the only acupuncturist in your town still gives you a great advantage in introducing yourself to your community.

To help give you an idea of what areas have the least competition you can use some research tools available on the web. Acupuncture Today has a useful tool on their website—a density map—that shows the number of acupuncturists (at least those subscribing to Acupuncture Today) in each state by the first three numbers in their zip code: www.acupuncturetoday.com/list/info/aculocatorzip/

You can then check the population in those zip codes with a website for the U.S. Census Bureau: http://factfinder.census.gov/home/saff/main.html?_lang=en

Another tool that can be helpful in your research is the search engine at Acufinder.com. This site lists most all practitioners for free and then offers expanded listings for a fee. The search is done by entering a zip code and then how many miles a radius from that zip code to search. This search resource is not only helpful for learning about the number of practitioners in whatever area you are researching, but the expanded listings often have practitioner's websites and information about the practitioner. This is a great place to scope-out your competition including getting website ideas.

In the year 2000, I was helping out the people of the insurance company American Specialty Health (ASH) to develop their network of providers in various states. In order for managed care plans to be approved, most states require that the insurance company has a network of providers that can allow policy holders reasonable access—close enough that they won't have to drive too far to find an approved provider. ASH needed more acupuncturists in the state of Idaho to contract with them to meet Idaho's requirement for provider access. ASH was going to have several meetings there for prospective providers and I offered to make calls to several acupuncturists in the less populated areas to let them know about these meetings and see if they would be interested in attending. I was a bit surprised to find out most of the acupuncturists I spoke to were too busy to be interested in becoming providers. They didn't really need the business. I only spoke to a modest number of these acupuncturists and it was by no means a scientific survey like those showing so many acupuncturists struggling. Even so, it suggested to me that being one of the few acupuncturists in even modestly populated, conservative leaning areas can work-out.

Some of you reading this may be thinking that you would never consider moving to another state or even another town to give yourself a better chance of building a successful practice and that brings up a bigger issue of just how motivated those who enter this profession are. In my introduction, I quoted some pretty dismal statistics about how poorly most acupuncturists are doing in their new careers. Much of this book has taken the position that there should be plenty of work—plenty of patients—for all of us if we as a profession and you as an individual practitioner had the right knowledge regarding the realities of private practice. While I still believe this to be true my opinion in this regard assumes that practitioners are willing to do whatever it takes to build a successful practice.

One subject that seldom seems to come up within our profession is the question of the level of dedication those who become licensed have to making a career out of their chosen field. The only one I have seen address this is Lisa Rohldener of the Community Acupuncture Network who has probably spoken to more acupuncturists about building private practices or those seeking employment than anybody in our profession. Lisa laments that many people coming out of our schools have little idea how hard (and smart) one has to work to either make it in private practice or become an asset to an employer. Contrast the average acupuncture/OM graduate to those becoming medical physicians. Those entering medical school will often move to find the school that works best for them and also then be ready to go just about anywhere to begin their careers. Once they start practicing, physicians work very long hours. A study published in a 2010 edition of the Journal of the American Medical Association found that from the years 1996 to 2008, physicians had reduced their average work hours from 55 hours a week to 51. I am not sure how many acupuncturists starting their practices are ready to work 50+ hours a week, but if you want to give yourself the best chance to build a private practice those are the types of hours you had better be prepared to work.

It may be that a good percentage of those entering the A/OM profession are not looking to make a full-blown career out of it and that they just want to work part time. Of course that is fine and I hope the information provided in this book will help you accomplish what you wish to accomplish in your involvement in this field. However, for those who got into this profession expecting to make a career out of it, I hope you can appreciate that it does take long hours to give you the best chance to be successful. There are exceptions no doubt, but serious practice building is a full-time endeavor.

If you decide to open your practice in an area saturated with other acupuncturists, take some time to learn about their practice. Are they all doing general practice or are some of them specializing in treating certain conditions? This could be the best situation to specialize yourself. In the following chapter, I offer advice on some of the many specialized areas acupuncture has applications in. If you decide on an area of specialization, you should especially contact the conventional health care providers that work in that field and try to establish a relationship with them as I describe in the next chapter. You should also contact the local acupuncturists and let them know you are opening your specialized practice and are looking to establish relationships with other A/OM practitioners you could refer to when patients outside your area of specialization need that care.

Whatever town you decide to settle in, you also need to decide where you will situate your practice. Some practitioners decide to practice out of their home to save the cost of leasing office space. Although I am certainly supportive of trying to keep overhead as low as reasonably possible, I strongly advise you to find suitable office space and not try to practice out of your home. Unless you live in a very rural area where other professionals like medical doctors practice out of their homes, having an acupuncture practice in your home sends all the wrong signals to the public. You want to show the public that you are a licensed health care professional and most licensed health care professionals work out of professional buildings.

One of the tougher decisions you will face regarding finding office space is how much to spend for what type of location. Space in a building on the corner of a busy intersection that gets plenty of drive-by and walk-by traffic will cost more than a similar space in a building with little or no traffic or visibility. As I write this, we are deep into a recession that has seen many businesses close and a great deal of office space is vacant and prices have dropped. This being the case, you may be able to afford a better space with better visibility and traffic than just a few years ago. There is no magic formula about how to figure the trade-off of how much more to spend to get better visibility, but if you are just starting out, I still advise that you should look to go with less expensive space. It may be that the more expensive, higher visibility office more than pays for itself by attracting lots of patients and keeping other advertising costs low, but it is a gamble. Start off with as low an overhead as possible while still finding professional looking space and give yourself time to build a patient base before thinking of moving into a higher-priced building.

In addition to considering the location of office space, there are some basic features of an office space you will want to consider. Avoid buildings in run-down areas of town or that would in any way convey a negative impression. You want to build the public's confidence that you are a respectable health care professional and the look of your office will make an important first impression. You should look at the parking situation and if the building has easy access including being wheelchair accessible. You will be best off with a ground floor office but if not on the ground floor make sure there is an elevator and that it will not be too big of a burden to people in wheelchairs or those using walkers. Treating elderly patients can be a significant part of your practice and having good access is especially important to this group and even some of your younger patients will have difficulty ambulating so keep that in mind.

You also want to make sure that your office space has a dedicated wash facility. Do not get an office in which you must go out your front door into the building's common area corridor to get into a restroom. You need to wash your hands before touching your patients and so having wash facilities available to you in your own office is essential. You don't need to have a sink in every treatment room, but you do need one within your office space. What I have done in my last two offices is to put a second sink in the treatment room that abuts the restroom. It does not cost much money to have this done as the plumbing lines are close and you might be able to get your landlord to do this as part of your lease. It really helps to have that second sink in case someone is in your restroom when you are getting ready to wash before going into a treatment room but even if a second sink is not feasible for you, you need to have one inside your office.

I strongly advise against relying on hand sanitizer solutions rather than washing your hands. While these solutions have been accepted as a substitute for hand washing in some circles and they certainly have their place, a private practice acupuncture office is not the right place for the use of those solutions. The Centers for Disease Control only accepted these solutions after becoming frustrated in their campaign to get doctors in hospitals to always wash their hands between patients. Your patients will think more highly of you when they see you always washing your hands before touching them. I have had many patients tell me how impressed they were at the fact that I was constantly washing my hands. In California, washing hands before performing acupuncture is required by statute and the insurance company American Specialty Health who has the nation's largest network of contracted acupuncturists requires dedicated hand-washing facilities to join their network.

Another consideration when selecting an office is how much space you will need. If you are just starting out I recommend you keep the square footage down. My first office was about 400 square feet, my next one was about 900 square feet and my current office is about 1400 square feet. In my first office, I used two treatment tables and had them divided by a set of curtains. This was OK but I much prefer to have separate treatment rooms as I have had in my last offices. My advice is that having 500-600 square feet with two treatment rooms is probably sufficient to get started. With the real estate market in such a low point now you might find a larger space at a great price and that might work out great for you but also give thought to how much more it may take you to pay for utilities and other monthly maintenance expenses. You might find a space twice as large as another that is going for about the same monthly lease rate and think it a great bargain but when you consider utilities and maintenance it could add considerable costs.

When I signed the lease for my first office space, I had never done such a thing before. I had no experience with leases or contracts and was very fortunate that the man who owned the building was a good guy who dealt fairly with me. You can't count on that always being the case though. While I now have more experience with leases, I am not an expert and I am certainly not a real estate attorney that can give you legal advice about leases. I will share some of what I have learned about this subject but encourage you to also get further advice. One thing you should seriously consider while looking for office space is to work with a commercial real estate agent or broker. Just as when you are buying a house and use a buyer's real estate agent to help you find houses and negotiate a purchase contract, there are commercial agents that do the same for those looking for office space. They also work off a commission figured as a percentage of the value of the lease you sign. It may be a little difficult to find such an agent to work too hard for you if you are looking for a small space at a low price but it is still worthwhile to try. A good agent will know the properties in their areas and can help you negotiate the terms of the lease in a way that looks out for your best interest.

As many property owners are hurting now with more and more vacancies, you might be able to find very favorable terms. While a commercial real estate agent can explain things to you better than I can, it helps to understand that commercial properties like office buildings and retail spaces are valued by the amount of income they produce. This being the case, property owners often prefer to have lease terms that charge more per month but perhaps give several months in free rent to start rather than charging a lower monthly fee with no free rent. However the lease gets structured, just know that many things are negotiable. Owners may pay for construction to fix-up the space the way you need it. They usually will not give any break on the maintenance cost of the common areas of the building called "common area maintenance" or "CAM" fees. CAM fees cover the owner's costs for maintaining the common areas of the building including landscaping and lighting and may include things like insurance and property taxes.

Make sure that when you are looking at the cost per square foot for office space that you also find out what the CAM charges are. Some buildings may have a low cost per square foot but high CAM charges. These fees are calculated by what percentage of the building your space occupies so the CAM fees are an additional fee per square foot to what you will be paying for your space.

As an example of some things to consider when comparing office space; a 500 square foot (sq. ft.) space leasing for $1.00 per sq. ft. with a $.50 a sq. ft. CAM charges brings the actual cost to $1.50 a sq. ft. A 500 sq. ft. space at $1.50 a sq. ft. will cost $750 per month. Another space may lease for $1.20 a sq. ft. and have a $.20 a sq. ft. CAM charges and this would make a total of $1.40 per sq. ft. totaling $700 per month. This being the case, the office with the $1.20 per sq. ft. rent actually ends-up being less expensive than the one charging $1.00 per sq. ft. Make sure you understand all of the charges associated with your lease. In California, we have regulations that keep property taxes near what they were when the owner first bought the building and then these are reassessed to the current value when the building changes hands. If your lease requires you to pay a share of these taxes and the building has been owned a long time and so the taxes are lower than current value, you should have a stipulation in your lease that your share of taxes will not increase if the building is sold.

Just as important as the cost of the rent and any additional fees like CAM charges is the length of time of your lease. A lease is a contract that you sign legally obligating you and the owner to the terms of the contract. The owner (or their agent) will want you to sign for a longer term and will likely be willing to offer better terms for a longer lease but you need to be careful about longer-term obligations. If you agree to a long-term lease and then decide you don't like the building or are having trouble staying in business, the owner can demand you continue to pay as you agreed to do. A very good middle ground is to agree to a shorter initial term with an option to renew the lease after that term expires. Instead of signing a five year lease for example, offer to do a one or two year with a four or three year option. Again, these types of details are the things a good commercial agent can help you with but if you can't find one do some research. Go online and look for resources offering advice on signing a lease. It is also a very good idea to talk to other people in the building you are interested in and ask them what their experience has been with the management. You should also check with your professional association as offering advice on subjects like negotiating leases is yet another subject that your professional association should be able to provide.

Whatever location and size of office you choose, it is vital that you make sure your office is *clean*. You need to impress upon people that you are a solid health care professional and nothing will hurt that image more than a shabby office. Just how you decorate your office can vary depending on your overall marketing efforts. I think practitioners should style their office as a reflection of their own style. Some acupuncturists will want to portray themselves similar to medical doctors and wear white lab coats. If this is the case, your office should reflect this in its décor. Other acupuncturists may want to express the Asian influence in this medical system while still others will go for a laid-back, perhaps even New Age vibe. Whatever your style, make sure you keep your office clean. Cleanliness goes with any décor and helps combat negative stereotypes of acupuncturists as being unprofessional. I have never used a cleaning service but then again, when I was a teenager I had a job cleaning office buildings. Between my wife and myself we manage to keep our office looking good with less than 30 minutes a week of work. I even sometimes clean our carpets myself although we have a patient who has a carpet cleaning business that we trade treatments with too. The bottom line here is that it does not have to cost you much to keep your office clean and doing so is important to how your patients perceive you.

Speaking of cleanliness, make sure you regularly clean your treatment tables and work surfaces with a disinfectant-type cleaner such as Lysol. If your table has a face plate or facial slot, you need to clean this with disinfectant after each use even when using a cover. You don't want patient after patient putting their faces in these rests without cleaning them each time they are used. You should also make sure you spray the floor area below a face plate or face slot as people will tend to drool especially if they fall asleep during the treatment. Not very glamorous I know, but this is all part of the job.

Among some of the other considerations you will want to give to your office set-up is making sure your patients are as comfortable as possible during the treatment. As I mentioned earlier, this is important not only because it is a nice thing to do but the more comfortable your patients are the better the treatment will work. One of the best pieces of equipment you can have to help in this regard is the body cushion pad. These pads are especially useful when you have a patient lie face down when doing points on the back surface of the body. As these pads come with a face plate, you will need a treatment table that has a facial slot in it. Tables that have a face rest that you slide into place at the end of the table will not work when using these pads so give that some thought when buying your treatment tables. Once a patient is in position on this pad, you then slide a pillow under their ankles to complete the position. Some pads will come with a wedge pad for this.

One challenge in using these pads is getting your patient into and out of them comfortably. Although they are adjustable for patients of different heights, some obese patients might have trouble fitting into them and those with severe back or neck pain will especially have difficulty getting out of this position without straining themselves. As patients can often be lightheaded when first rising after a treatment, it is better if you can help them up or at least stand by to make sure they do not get too dizzy when getting up from the pad especially for elderly or otherwise frail patients.

Another very useful piece of equipment is the TDP or far-infrared lamp devices. These are very useful to help relax muscles and improve circulation and patients love them. You do need to be careful with them, however, as they have the potential for causing burns if placed too close to the skin or if they are touched while hot. While I don't have specific statistics of this, in the work I have done with the insurance industry, complaints from patients regarding burns, either from these types of lamps or various moxa therapies, are probably the most frequently seen reasons. They are so helpful I would never be without them but be careful in how you use them.

Another consideration in setting up your office is the safe management and disposal of disposable needles. Once acupuncture needles are used they need to be placed in an appropriate container that is securely out of the reach of children and then properly disposed of. There are two main systems for disposing used needles. One is paying for a pick-up service that comes into your office and picks-up the used container and the other is a mail-back system. In the mail-back system you purchase a container and pay extra for the cost of a shipping container and disposal. Once the container is full, you box it up and mail it back to the company you bought it from and they dispose of it. Until you start to see a lot of patients, the cost of needle disposal should not be much at all as it takes a long time to fill those containers. Whatever you do, follow the law with regard to needle disposal. Don't throw used needles in the trash. Not only is it illegal, it is a public hazard. People who handle trash as part of their job have enough difficulties without having to worry about being stuck with a used acupuncture needle because some idiot acupuncturist was too cheap to dispose of their needles properly.

One of the most important things you can do in building a practice from scratch is to strive to have all telephone calls answered by a live person. When you are first trying to establish yourself, you don't want to let any call go to an answering machine if you can avoid it. If people are making their first call to your office and are already nervous about seeking acupuncture services, you want to have their calls answered by a friendly, professional, and knowledgeable source. This can be tricky as it likely won't be affordable to hire a receptionist at first (more on this in Chapter 20) and this means answering the phone yourself.

There are also answering services available that will give callers some basic information and then fax or email you reports. These services can start as for as little as $30 per month for up to 50 calls plus a little for each report. If you find you are missing calls and people are not leaving messages, such a service would be worth it. You would only forward your calls to such a service during business hours otherwise people expect an answering machine during off hours. On both your answering machine and any script you give an answering service to use, make sure you mention that callers can go to your website to get more information. You should also do this when you are talking to people who call. While you want to give them useful information, you should not let them ask question after question just for the sake of talking. It is one thing to answer the phone yourself, answer a few pertinent questions, let them know you offer a free, no obligation consultation where you can give more information and then direct them to your website for further information, but don't spend more than five minutes. If they want that much of your time, they should come in for the consultation. If they want to talk longer and don't want to set-up a consultation, they are not serious and not worth your time.

I worked my office by myself for the first two or three years and did just fine. The first receptionist I hired was a patient of mine. I paid her minimum wage and she worked 4 hours, three days a week. We would schedule the modest patient load to be more clustered around her hours when possible. When I moved to a bigger office with an extra treatment room, I was approached by a massage therapist who was just starting out and wanted to know if she could work for me. I told her I needed a receptionist more than a massage therapist but, if she worked for me at minimum wage 20-25 hours a week, I would help her get her massage business going. She eventually got busy enough that she was able to stop the receptionist work and pay me for the treatment room space. My point in sharing my experiences with staff is to emphasize that you can find affordable ways to get help when you are busy enough to need it. While finding the right person and making it work financially is not easy, with some creative effort it does not have to be too expensive.

Dress And Manner

I highly suggest you strive to dress professionally and to present yourself in such a manner that does not suggest trying to look sexually attractive. For female practitioners, this means using conservative make-up and non-flattering attire. For males, again, wear conservative, non-flattering attire. If you wear a lab coat, that makes the dress issue a bit easier. It is just an unfortunate reality that working as a healthcare professional that touches people leaves one open to patients who can misconstrue such contact. This is even more of a problem for male practitioners, especially since most A/OM practitioners will not be able to have a female assistant with them when they are with the patient at all times. My advice to both male and female practitioners is to never compliment patients of the opposite sex about their looks. If your patient has lost weight, you can say they look healthier, but don't say anything that suggests you think they look attractive. Also be very careful about hugs. I might hug or compliment the looks of one of my eighty or ninety year old female patients but not with other age groups. Doing so only invites trouble.

CHAPTER NINETEEN

Getting Them In Your Door

Ask most acupuncturists what they believe to be the biggest obstacle keeping people from seeking-out acupuncture and they will probably tell you it is the fear of needles. No one likes being stuck with needles and people just don't understand that modern acupuncture needles are so thin that being stuck with one is not like being stuck with any other type of needle. It is no doubt true that the acupuncture profession faces a difficult chore in getting people to be comfortable with the idea of being stuck with several needles as a form of therapy but I have long-felt that the fear of needles is not our profession's biggest challenge. If you think of this issue from a different angle, the fear of needles really translates to a lack of confidence in acupuncturists.

Why do I think the fear of needles actually masks an underlying lack of confidence in acupuncturists? Because far more people go to dentists and dental hygienists than go to acupuncturists even though most people would find the idea of letting someone drill into their teeth or dig around their gums to be even more scary than being stuck with needles. The difference between dentists and acupuncturists is that most people have learned to trust that dentists are well-trained and professional enough to manage the discomfort and make their procedures tolerable. The acupuncture profession has not yet achieved this level of the public's trust. It is not that people think acupuncturists are untrustworthy; they know nothing at all about acupuncturists—even the fact that acupuncturists have to be licensed to practice. The issue is less about the pain of being stuck with needles and more about not trusting the professionalism of those who do the needle-sticking. It is the fear of the unknown.

Considering that most people know nothing at all about what type of training acupuncturists get or even what kind of person tends to become an acupuncturist, the most important obstacle we as a profession and you as a private practitioner face is educating the public about acupuncturists. This being the case, the best way to help get patients in your door is to do everything you can to introduce yourself as a caring, intelligent, professional. Ask most people what they think of when you say the word "acupuncturist" and not many are going to answer "caring, intelligent, professional." Most will not know what to say or maybe they will think of some mysterious or New Age stranger, not someone they could personally relate to like they could relate to a dentist. You need to change that by employing a well thought-out marketing campaign.

Marketing

There are many methods that you can apply to introduce yourself to your local market and attract people to your practice. We will consider several marketing methods in this section but first we should consider some of the general realities of marketing your practice and yourself. A smart marketing campaign needs to find the delicate balance between spending enough to attract patients by introducing yourself to your market and not spending too much that could make you go broke before you get your practice going. It takes time to get your name or your clinic's name in peoples' minds and often people who are interested in contacting you will procrastinate for months before making contact. If you are going to place ads in the local newspaper for example, don't judge the success of the ad by how many calls you get the day or two after the ad runs. It just doesn't work that way. Marketing is a cumulative process. Your challenge is to survive in practice long enough to allow that accumulation to take place. It usually takes a good two to three years before the cumulative effect of your marketing efforts will start to reach their full potential so be careful about spending a lot of money on advertising early-on if money is tight.

In order to find that balance between under spending and overspending, you should set yourself a budget for how much you can afford to pay for marketing. Your marketing budget will of course be part of your overall budget for things like rent, utilities, supplies and so forth. You should have this budget estimated before you sign a lease or make any big decisions about opening your practice. Once you have a marketing budget in mind, you should then try to get as creative as you can about how to get the most out of that budget. Considering that it will take two to three years for the money you spend to reach its full potential, look at your marketing plan as a long-range one in which you try to do what you can to generate some short-term referrals while waiting for the cumulative process to build.

As we will consider, there is a lot you can do to help introduce yourself to your local market that does not have to cost much money. When you first open your practice, you are going to have some free time on your hands. This will seem like your biggest problem—not having enough patients to work on and sitting around waiting for the phone to ring or someone to walk in your door. True, it is a problem you must work to solve, but like most things in life, there are benefits to the downside of having spare time like this. You should look to make this time as productive as possible especially by using this time to brainstorm about how to better practice your art and how to market yourself. Don't sit around feeling sorry for yourself. If you do achieve the blessing of building a busy practice, you will end-up with the problem of not having enough time to read some of the Chinese medicine books you would like or to give talks to local groups or work on your website. Take advantage of the extra time when you have it. If you practice Qi-Gong or Tai-Chi or any meditative arts, practicing these also helps refine your qi and makes you a better practitioner. I miss not having as much time as I did in my first years of practice to do these activities.

Finally, before we consider some of the different marketing methods you can use to attract patients to your practice, I want to warn you to be prepared for something that caught me by surprise when I first opened my practice. Many businesses make their living by offering services to new businesses. They may find you by means of your new Yellow Pages listings or when you register your business with the local authorities, etc. However it is they do it, you will get a lot of calls, letters, e-mails, and people dropping by your office offering you fantastic ways for you to market your new business or buy your supplies. Some of these will be local groups like schools or Little League teams that will try to guilt you into advertising with them. Some of these may actually be worthwhile and we will consider a few of these later but there is no way you can or should advertise with them all. The best thing you can do is be firm and let them know that you have a very limited marketing budget and you already have that strategy laid out and can't partake in their offering at this time. Just don't get too disappointed when the phone rings or someone comes in your door and it turns out to be a salesperson instead of a prospective patient. You should also not get upset with them as I have actually had a few of these salespeople turn into patients or refer other patients even though I did not buy what they were selling.

Yellow Pages

It used to be that the Yellow Pages was the most important advertising many businesses could have. Many businesses owners named their businesses so they would be seen sooner in the Yellow Pages alphabetical listings such as "Acme" this or "Advanced" that. Nowadays, many more people are using internet searches rather than the Yellow Pages and so having a good website is even more important for building a practice than spending a lot of money on yellow page advertising. However, you still need to be listed in your local Yellow Pages but just be careful about how much money you spend on those ads. Look at your local Yellow Pages and see what your competition is doing. If you live in a large city with lots of competition, it may be true that a small ad might not get noticed but because large ads are so expensive, the extra exposure of a large ad will probably not be cost effective to someone starting out. If you live in a location where there is only a handful of other practitioners, having a big ad may make your practice stand out more but that still may not be worth the money because people looking for an acupuncturist will tend to call at least a few before making a decision to schedule an appointment with one. This being the case, worrying about what happens when people call your office is much more important than having a big Yellow Page ad.

Even before you open your office, you should check into the local Yellow Pages resources and find out just how their advertising zones are organized. In most locations, you will want to be listed in those books that service the areas all around your office with your office like a bull's-eye of a target. When I opened my first office, I did not realize that in order for my Yellow Page listing to reach the areas around my office, I would have to be listed in three different zones because I was located right at a border between zones. If you are looking at two different office locations and one is on the border of these zones and another is in the middle of a zone that would cover the areas you want to reach, understanding this might help in your decision of which office to choose. Either way, looking into the Yellow Pages zones will help you understand how much your Yellow Pages advertising will cost you.

Make sure your Yellow Pages advertising features your website address. It is far more cost effective to use your Yellow Pages advertisement to direct people to your website than to try to cram a lot of information about your practice in it. You should also seriously consider having your picture in this ad as humanizing the practice of acupuncture is so important to making people feel comfortable about trying it. Make sure you highlight that you offer a free (complimentary) initial consultation and that you accept insurance (if you are following my practice model and doing so).

Your Website

A website allows you to tell prospective patients not just about the services you offer but about you as a person. Most forms of advertising like the Yellow Pages or direct marketing are so expensive that you cannot afford to give much information in these mediums. It makes far more sense for most practitioners to focus a good part of their advertising budget on advertising their websites. Have your website address on your business cards, Yellow Page ad, and any other methods you use to get your practice name out there. This allows people to research you and your practice while giving you the chance to go into much more detail with little, if any, additional costs.

In my new office, I finally have a sign that can be seen but all my previous offices did not because of city codes. It helped that I had a small lawn type sign made with my website address and I would stick in the planter box in front of my office each morning. I still do even in my new office. Technically, this violates my city's sign code but it only cost me $30 so it would not be a big loss if the city ever made me take it down although that has not happened yet in over eight years in 2 offices. If your city will allow it, consider making your office sign double as an ad for your website by adding .com after it. If your clinic's name is "Springfield Acupuncture" and your website is www.SpringfieldAcupuncture.com, when you have your "Springfield

Acupuncture" sign made, add a small .com at the end and this will let people know about your website.

There are many resources for developing websites out there and I am looking to identify some that I could recommend to others starting out. Check my website for information on my efforts in this regard. Whatever you do about your site, make sure it gives people information about your education and licensing as well as showing at least one good picture of you. It can also be helpful to mention if you have children or how long you have lived in the area you practice in (if you have lived there long). You want to let people know you are a neighbor who wants to help them with their problems and has the training to do so. Strip away the mystery of both the practice and the practitioner. Acupuncture is a therapy that stimulates self healing and while the methods of doing so are many and can be complex, you have undergone a great deal of training to be able to perform this therapy safely and effectively. You should also make sure the copy (wording) on your site has been carefully proof-read. Having typos and poor sentence structure can ruin what might have been good content. I may be able to recommend some resources for that also.

Most website experts stress the need to make sure your website ranks high in search engines. For an acupuncture practice, doing the things that helps a website get higher rankings in search engines is not so important if you are in an area with little competition. Most search engines will read the Internet Service Provider (ISP) address nearest you so when someone enters "acupuncture" in their search engine; it will give listings for acupuncture websites and practices in that area. If you are one of only a few acupuncturists in town and someone does a search for acupuncture, your site will come up as one of the first sites. Often, people searching for an acupuncturist will also enter the name of the town they hope to find an acupuncturist in. That is why it can be a good idea to name your practice and website after your town such as "Springfield Acupuncture" and your site as www.SpringfieldAcupuncture.com. If a potential patient lives in Springfield and searches "acupuncture Springfield", your site will be very near if not at the very top.

Ranking high on search engines is much more of a concern if you live in an area with lots of competition. While the systems the search engines use to calculate rankings are always being adjusted, most authorities say adding new content regularly is very important. The more your site is a "content" site with useful information rather than a commercial site, the higher it will rank. Again, if you can name your practice and site after your town, doing so will put you up high in your local search engines but if that name is taken by another acupuncturist, you can add something to the title. For example, if another practice already has "Springfield Acupuncture" you can name your practice "Springfield Wellness and Acupuncture Center." Or, if you are going to market your practice by some angle of specialization, you might use "Acupuncture Pain Clinic of Springfield" or "Acupuncture Fertility Center of Springfield", or something similar.

Many acupuncturists name their practices based on their philosophy or style or practice with names like "Caring Hands Acupuncture" or "Spiritual Axis Acupuncture" etc. While names like these may help identify the special niche you see yourself as occupying, they don't work well from a marketing perspective. They don't help your search engine rankings and usually are not easy for people to remember or even understand. I made this mistake in my first office when I named it "Holistic Care Center." It only confused the public and people did not remember it when they went to tell their friends about me. The two best options when naming your office and website are to either name it after the town or location of your office as we have considered or name it after yourself. Naming your office after your name like "Mary Brown, L.Ac. Acupuncture" may not work as well on search engine rankings as using your town's name but at least it focuses people on you as the caregiver. You could do a hybrid of your name and that of your town such as "MaryBrownSpringfieldAcupuncture". Of course, you probably only want to use your name like this if you are working as a solo practitioner.

The one drawback to naming your practice after your town is if you later decide to move to another town you will lose that name recognition and will have to start over again. This being the case, using your name in combination with your town is a good idea if you might be moving to another town before too long. This should still help your search rankings while featuring your name so if you later move to a nearby town, you can just switch the towns' name for your new practice and website and people who got to know you by your name can still find you and refer their friends by mentioning your name.

Whatever you decide to do about the name of your office and website, you should spend more time figuring out how to introduce yourself personally and advertise your web site address rather than spending too much time worrying about search engine rankings. If you had to choose between going to a local business mixer to introduce yourself and hand out business cards with your web address on them or sitting at a computer trying to write more content for your site in the hopes of higher search rankings, go to the mixer! If you have time to do both that is fine but being that you are a service provider and not selling products, making personal connections is more important than search engine rankings. Besides, most people looking for an acupuncturist will look at more than just the first ranking site in their search. They will look to find one that is close to them and then who they feel comfortable with once they do some research on a few sites. As long as your site comes up in the top five or six for your area you should be fine.

Personal Networking

Spend a lot of time brainstorming on different ways you can introduce yourself to your community. I will offer advice on how to introduce yourself to other healthcare professionals later in this chapter but let's first consider other ways to do this with the general public. Much of what I will be suggesting here has to do with personal networking and giving talks or classes. For those of you who are uncomfortable with public speaking, you should consider working on improving your skills in that area. Your chances of building a successful practice will be much better if you do. You are going to have to learn how to explain acupuncture to your patients anyway so with some practice, you should be able to do the same to small groups of people.

Joining your local Chamber of Commerce can often be useful for networking opportunities as well as business resources and advice. If you join, don't just do so to have your practice listed in their directory but rather to take advantage of as many of their services as you can. You can also try to find out about other business networking groups active in your area. You should dress professionally when you attend these functions and always remember to have plenty of business cards with you to hand out.

Another way to introduce yourself to your community is to go to local businesses especially health food stores, hair or nail salons, really any sort of business that caters to health and beauty markets. You can just pop into these, give a quick introduction, offer your card and make sure you let them know your card has your web address where they can get more information and then ask if they would mind you leaving more cards in case they have any customers or friends that might be interested. Of course, you should be mindful not to interrupt them if they are with a client and be very quick about it while also being happy to take the time answer any questions they may have. Most everyone will not refuse you offering them your business card even if they are going to throw it in the trash as soon as you walk out. Offer them the one card first and then quickly say you would be happy to leave more if they would like but don't show any offense if they tell you they don't want any additional cards. Just thank them and get out the door. This should not take more than one minute unless they are interested and want more information.

Online Social Networking

There are so many new tools available on the internet that can be used to help you make a personal connection with your local market. It is not just about going to mixers or giving talks any more although I still believe those face-to-face venues are the best way for people to get to know you and feel comfortable with seeking your services. Hosting a blog and online social networking resources such as Facebook, Twitter, Myspace, etc., offer opportunities that did not exist when I opened my practice 25 years ago. I have to confess, I don't know these mediums well at all and I don't use them so I can't offer you specific advice on how to use them. I would just give you this general advice that holds true for any marketing plan and that is that you are trying to present yourself as a caring, intelligent, professional so make sure that anything associated with your name does not contradict that image.

Cross Marketing By Holding Classes

One really helpful approach you can take in your marketing is to consider holding some sort of classes such as in acupressure techniques, herbs, Chinese diet therapy, or Tai Chi or Qi-Gong. Developing these types of services that are different from your practice yet also related to it is employing a technique known as "cross-marketing." The best type of cross-marketing is done by offering things that attract people with different interest. Some people who might never think of going to an acupuncturist for acupuncture might be very interested in taking a class on Chinese herbs or diet therapy for example. Once they attend this class and get to know you and see you are an intelligent and caring person, they may then be much more open to seeing you for acupuncture especially after they learn more about it from you. Also, some of your patients who come to you for acupuncture might never have thought about attending a class on herbs but they may develop that interest after learning about your classes while seeing you for treatment.

Early in my practice building years, I held some classes at a local community college on acupressure. I taught a dozen or so points but also taught people how to do some basic auricular acupressure using pressure spheres. This was really popular as it is so easy to learn and gets pretty consistent results. Several of those people who attended this class also became patients of mine and a few of those patients referred many more to me over the years. A good strategy for those types of classes is to make them a three or four part class in which you charge a modest amount per class but then give a discount if they sign-up for all the classes. This allows people to just pay for the first class and then if they like it they can sign-up for the rest and get a discount.

What worked out so nicely about this acupressure class was that the community college had its own marketing for its classes so I did not have to spend any money to market it other than fliers I handed out in my office. Even if you don't have such a resource available to you, you can hold small classes in your office. You might even do these for free at first. Just ask your patients who are interested in attending to please bring a friend. Or, you could charge a small fee for the class if a patient attends alone and waive that fee if they bring a friend. You should also post that you have classes on your website and that people should e-mail you if they want to attend.

Chinese medicine has compiled the world's greatest body of natural healing wisdom. Those who have studied this system of health care have learned a great deal of valuable information and people will be interested in what you have to offer if you put together the right types of classes and market them well. This is a natural fit for cross-marketing. Some acupuncturists might even be able to grow this aspect of their business larger than their practice if they really apply themselves.

Even if all you do is offer a few small classes a year, doing this can be a great means of cross marketing and help you establish yourself more quickly than just offering acupuncture treatment. This can be especially important in those first few years while trying to survive long enough to establish yourself and while you have spare time.

Other Forms of Advertising

A very inexpensive way to help get your practice's name out to the public is to use magnetic cars signs. These signs are removable and a pair of them can run from about $50 to $100. As always, make sure they contain your web site address as well as your phone number. Of course, it is best to use these on a nice, clean car and not a junker. You should also remove any bumper stickers with political or religious hot-button messages on them. Make sure you always have plenty of your business cards in the car to hand out if anyone asks about your practice. An even less expensive way to do a little marketing with your car is with customized license place frames. Place your website address and office phone number on the frame. Every little bit helps.

Most communities will have local publications that have advertising rates that are not too expensive. Such publications as the Thrifty Nickel or Pennysaver are delivered free either in the mail or given away at retail locations. You can usually place a small ad in these types of publications for a reasonable rate. As mentioned in the beginning of this section on marketing, you don't run these types of ads and expect them to generate calls to your office right away. These types of ads are best used as a long-term means of creating name recognition for your practice. The best way to get the most cost-effective use of these types of ads is to run them for about four consecutive weeks, take off a month or two and then run them again for another four weeks. When people see your ad more than once in a row, it sticks in their minds better than if you were to run it every other week.

I warned you earlier in this section that once you open your practice, you will likely be bombarded by salespeople offering you marketing opportunities. Some of those would include things like placing ads in a local high schools program for a school play, or placing a sign at the Little League playing field or golf course, or a local supermarket offering some sign space on their shopping carts. You may hear from the local police association or Boy or Girl Scouts. Many of these ads will not cost much money but their penetration in your market will also be quite limited. I think the way you can get the most out of these very specialized ads is to choose one or two if they are ones you have some personal connection with. If you have children playing in Little League and you go to the games, then having a sign for your practice at the playing field makes much more sense than if you don't have that connection with that advertisement's intended audience. If you are marketing yourself as specializing in sports medicine then having an ad at the local golf course or in the high school's football program might be well worth the cost.

Being in the Yellow Pages, having and advertising your website, joining local networking groups or business groups, holding classes out of your office or local colleges or parks and recreation department, handing out cards to local businesses, running small ads in local Pennysaver or Thrifty Nickel type publications—all of these efforts start the multi-year process of building name recognition for you and your practice in your local community.

Health Care Professionals

In addition to introducing yourself to the general public of your community, you should also work at introducing yourself to the health/wellness and medical community in your area. This not only includes medical doctors, osteopaths, naturopaths, and chiropractors, but also physical therapists, massage therapists, dentists, health food stores, and any others out there providing some sort of health and wellness goods and services. While there are still skeptics that might not "believe" in acupuncture especially amongst some medical doctors, there will be those in all of the professions I listed above who have at least heard some good things about acupuncture. Many of these types have been asked by their own patients/clients about acupuncture and might not have anyone to whom they feel comfortable referring to. If you can introduce yourself to them and impress upon them that you seem like a reasonable, educated professional, they might well be happy to refer people to you although it usually takes some time to build the level of trust needed before this happens.

While I am trying to give advice on several different types of health care professionals, I can't cover every one that could be useful to connect with. Acupuncture has so many different applications in so many different fields of medicine. You need to give thought to what other types you could reach-out to. Developing a good working relationship with just one of these providers could mean the difference between surviving those first years or not. With acupuncture, you bring something to the table virtually no one else can offer – stimulating the body's own resources. It is a safe therapy and, if you charge on the modest side, it can be very affordable. In short, there is almost no reason why most all patients with most all kinds of problems wouldn't benefit from having acupuncture. The problem is that not many people including health care professionals realize this. Work at finding ways to get this message across without sounding like you are saying that you are a better practitioner or the services you provide are more valuable than those others.

It is vital that when you go about introducing yourself to any type of health care professional that you convey respect for what they do. Nobody is going to refer one of their patients to anyone who disrespects the services they themselves provide. This being the case, be careful in the way you promote your practice and refer to mainstream medicine or the medical profession. You also need to be sensitive about how these professionals will regard you and your request for them to consider you as a resource for their patients especially if they may see you as competition. When it comes to communicating with Medical Doctors and Osteopaths, you should stress that you have respect for what they do and that as acupuncture stimulates the patient's own internal resources it can be a perfect complement for modern medical therapies that utilize outside resources. You should also let them know that you are trying to establish contact not just to ask that they consider referring patients to you but because you need to find physicians to whom you can refer your patients. As with all of your marketing efforts, let them know they or their patients can look at your website to get more information but make sure your website does not have language that is critical of physicians or modern medicine as a whole.

When you communicate with Chiropractors, Naturopaths, and people like massage therapists, you will usually find them more sympathetic to what you do as these professions have also been somewhat persecuted or at least disrespected by mainstream medical authorities. However, with these types of practitioners, there will tend to be more overlap in the respective patient-base and even scope of practice and thus you might be seen as competing for the same patients. Find out if Chiropractors or Naturopaths are allowed to do acupuncture in your state before trying to connect with these practitioners in your area. If acupuncture is in their scope of practice, find out if those in your community are doing acupuncture. If they are, drop them a note letting them know that you are accepting new patients and that if they ever need to refer outside of their practice you would be happy to work with them to accommodate this. If they are not practicing acupuncture, let them know how well acupuncture can complement the therapies they provide and that you have studied with top specialists from China, Korea, or whatever applies in your case and mention any specialized training or focus of your practice that might not be in competition with them. If you offer treatment for quit smoking or fertility for example, these would not usually be the types of things most Chiropractors or some Naturopaths would commonly treat.

In offering the following advice on approaching these different types of health care professionals, one bit of generic advice can apply to how you approach all of them, especially those that seem hesitant of skeptical: After explaining how your services can complement theirs, suggest they consider referring one or two of their more difficult cases as a trial. You might even offer to see them for no charge although you should be careful to not sound to desperate in offering this. You just want to convey that you understand that referring some of their patients for acupuncture may seem too outside the box for them but you are so sure you can be of help that you are willing to be flexible to get the opportunity to show how you can help. Again, the tone you want to strike with this tactic is not desperation but of appreciating that the therapy you provide is so unusual in some peoples' eyes that you are willing to work with them to get the opportunity to show what you can do.

Overall, the biggest obstacle to overcome in getting health care professionals to refer to you is to win their trust that their patients will have a good experience under your care. Caring heath care professionals will feel a sense of responsibility for what happens to their patients when they refer them to someone else. The last thing they want is to have a patient come back and complain about having a bad experience with the provider they were referred to. Most would rather not refer at all if they have any doubts about what type of experience their patients will have so give this a lot of thought. Perhaps the best way to deal with this is to offer the health care professional a treatment so they can experience this for themselves. Just be mindful of how you make this offer. You are extending this courtesy because acupuncture is not well understood yet in the U.S. and you want to help them feel as comfortable as possible about referring to you.

Chiropractors:

Chiropractors can also be natural working partners with acupuncturists although there are probably more Chiropractors doing acupuncture in various states than any other type of health care professional. This being the case, you need to understand what the laws are regarding this in your state and also learn if the Chiropractors in your area are doing acupuncture and adjust your approach as I suggested above. In case you did not know, there is a fairly deep divide in the Chiropractic profession between those who believe Chiropractors should focus on treating orthopedic-type problems and others who promote Chiropractic as a broad type of holistic practice of helping the body to heal itself. Learning whether or not a Chiropractor you are looking to approach is in one camp or another can help you better tailor how you will describe what you can offer their patients.

Dentists:

Did you know that the dental profession was the first type of "conventional" modern physician to embrace acupuncture in the United States? When acupuncture first burst onto the scene here in the West in the 1970's, the application of acupuncture that caught everyone's attention was the way it was used in China for some surgeries in lieu of anesthesia. This especially interested the dental field as they often have patients who can't or don't want to use the anesthetic drugs used in some dental procedures. Many states allow dentists to perform acupuncture and a surprising number have at least tried this therapy in their practices and not just to replace the anesthetic drugs. Dentists often see patients for things like TMJ problems or even headaches when there is suspicion that dental problems might be at least partly responsible for the headaches.

I was recently at a family gathering and an old friend of the family was there who had just retired from a long practice as a dentist. He told me that he did some acupuncture in his practice and mentioned that he would have patients referred to him for headaches and jaw pain and he had found that acupuncture worked well with migraine headaches but he did not have as good of success with treating spasms in the jaw muscles. Perhaps if an acupuncturist would have made contact with him and impressed him that their more extensive training helped them to have better success with tough cases, this dentist might have been happy to refer those patients he was not successful with.

The most common conditions dentists will see in their practices that might be helped with acupuncture are headaches, TMJ or suspected TMJ-like problems, and trigeminal neuralgia as these conditions might have a dental component. If you have any experience with these conditions, let the dentists in your area know this and, as you should do with any type of health care provider, let them know you are also looking for people in their specialty to whom you could refer your patients.

Infertility specialists:

No other area of medicine in the last ten years has seen as much growth in the acceptance of acupuncture as is the case in fertility medicine. Studies showing acupuncture helped the success rates of I.V.F. procedures sparked this interest and this was fueled by internet fertility chat groups. There are now acupuncturists who specialize in this field and there is a specialty Board that has been formed to certify A/OM practitioners in Reproductive Medicine. This being the case, establishing yourself as having a specialty in A/OM fertility medicine can be a good strategy in many markets.

In a way, fertility patients are wonderful patients to have because their expectations tend to be far less than the average patient seen in A/OM practices. I don't mean to sound crass stating this, it is just a fact. Those involved in fertility issues have been repeatedly told there are no guarantees even with very expensive fertility clinics and with A/OM services, these patients are just looking for help in making the odds a little bit better. This takes some of the pressure off compared to the average patient. Another great feature of fertility clients is that they are so grateful if they are successful in having a child. In addition, these patients tend to be spending so much money already in fertility clinics that adding A/OM services tends to be a bargain for them. Lower than average stress to produce results, higher than average gratitude when successful, and less pressure about costs make these patients a good demographic to focus on for some newer practitioners.

There is a great deal of information on the subject of A/OM and fertility medicine and I suggest anyone interested in pursuing this as a specialty educate themselves about this field, especially the Western medical thinking so you will be better able to communicate with infertility specialists. Armed with a basic understanding of the Western terminology and physiology, you will be in a much better position to approach these specialists and offer to work with them.

Massage Therapists:

Massage therapists are another group that can provide a great resource for patient referrals. Many massage therapists have a lot of respect for acupuncture and will recommend their clients try acupuncture, especially the cases that are not responding well to their therapy. Over the years, I have treated a large number of the massage therapists in my area and I receive referrals from them regularly. I feel a bit awkward about this sometimes because I can't refer my patients to all of those massage therapists who are referring to me, but they seem to understand this. I will only refer to a massage therapist that I have received a massage from and whose techniques I like. Offering to do an exchange of treatments with massage therapists is a great way to build useful connections with them. This allows you to get an idea of their work and for them to do the same with you. Let them know you are looking for a massage therapist to refer to and offer an exchange as a way you can both get to know each other's styles of practice. If you find one or two you really like, make sure you also refer some of your patients to them on occasion.

Naturopaths:

Although Naturopaths are currently licensed in only about 15 states, I believe they have the potential to make very good working partners with acupuncturists. While their scope of practice varies quite a bit from state to state, in most states they can order lab tests and prescribe some medications while in a few states they can even do some surgery and/or deliver babies. In other words, they have the training and ability to do many aspects of Western medicine that Licensed Acupuncturists are not trained or licensed to do but they tend to be very supportive of acupuncture. In some states, Naturopaths are allowed to do acupuncture and various acupuncture organizations have been critical of this in the past and this has not made for great relations between these two professions. Other than these political turf battles between leaders of these groups, there would seem to be a natural synergy between Licensed Acupuncturists and Naturopaths. If you are in a state that licenses Naturopaths, make an extra effort to find one or more open to working with you. This could afford you the chance to refer your patients to someone who honestly supports the idea of natural healing but also has enough Western medical training to complement your services and vice versa.

OB/GYN:

Acupuncture, especially supplemented with the use of Chinese herbs, can be remarkably useful in a wide range of conditions that fall within the OB/Gyn realm. In fact, A/OM can be effective for such a wide range of these cases that most OB/Gyn physicians will find such claims hard to believe and you run the risk of not being taken seriously if you try to convince these physicians of this. My advice on the best way to approach these physicians is to not try to convince them of all that A/OM can due but focus instead on a few conditions that will seem more plausible.

The recent trials showing that hormone replacement therapy (HRT) caused more harm than was previously known have made the public leery about taking these drugs. As a result, these drugs are not being routinely used for treating menopausal symptoms except in extreme cases and this means many women suffering symptoms like hot flashes have less options available to them. Acupuncture alone can reduce these symptoms in most women and then if Chinese herbs are used in addition, the success rates go up even more. In early 2011, just as I was working on the final draft of this book, a study had been published and covered in the media reporting that acupuncture proved to be effective for treating hot flashes in postmenopausal women.

Keeping-up with such research can help you make a better case when approaching health care professionals.

You can try to explain to Gynecologists that because acupuncture helps the body to better balance its resources, this often has applications in improving hormone balance and that is why it sometimes improves IVF success rates. Let them know this can also be true for things like hot flashes and even cases like endometriosis.

As for Obstetricians, acupuncture (and moxa) has been shown in clinical trials to help turn breech babies and facilitate labor (although those trials showed mixed results for this). Unfortunately, it is not too often that any hospital or birthing center will let an acupuncturist try their treatments during the birthing process due to liability concerns. Despite this, I sometimes see patients who are due to deliver and not going into labor whose doctors tell them they will give them another few days before administering labor inducing drugs. Doing treatment in one's office to help induce labor is often successful and letting Obstetricians know this might get you some referrals.

Something most Obstetricians will have no idea of is that acupuncture can often help women with breast feeding issues especially if there is pain and or lack of milk issues. I recently saw a former patient of mine who had a child and developed a painful rash in her areola area that no one was able to help. She told me she had been to four different breast feeding consultants and none of their advice had worked. I asked her how many of those breast feeding consultants had advised her to use acupuncture. Of course, none of them had. Within three treatments the problem was a good 80% improved.

This breast feeding case, by the way, is a good example of what is so typical in A/OM practice. This was a former patient I had helped a couple of years before for a neck problem. She thought highly of me but did not think to consult me for the breastfeeding problem until after seeing several other types of health care professionals. There is no way acupuncturists can educate their patients about all the conditions acupuncture can treat by listing each one individually. That is why you need to stress that acupuncture helps the body to use its own resources and that your patients should contact you for virtually any problem so you can honestly tell them if you can help them. You want to keep stressing the point that you are an expert at helping their body to do a better job of helping itself and that has applications in most all health issues. I don't do as good a job of this with my patients as I could myself but I am not trying to stir-up more business. If all my patients really did consult me for every health issue they had, I could not handle the patient load. For those still building their practices however, educating your patients about how stimulating internal resources has remarkably broad applications will help you get many more patient visits out of less individual patients.

Orthopedic Physicians:

For most acupuncturists, patients with orthopedic (musculoskeletal) type problems represent the biggest percentage of their practices so connecting with Orthopedic Physicians can be crucial to practice building. I have included a sample letter here that you could use to send to some of the Orthopedic Physicians in your area. I will try to have this available for download at my website also. I suggest that any time you communicate with these doctors, you focus on explaining that acupuncture helps stimulate the body's natural pain relieving and anti-inflammatory chemistry and that this reduces pain and helps improve functioning significantly. You should also stress that this therapy has limits; it is not very effective in certain conditions such as when a nerve is being aggravated by bone spurs or disc fragments. Stressing the limits of acupuncture will make these physicians much more comfortable about working with you. The more such physicians sense you are exaggerating acupuncture's benefits, the less credibility you will have with them. You can suggest they consider referring some of their more difficult cases, especially those who may not be able to take stronger pain medications due to allergies or other medical conditions.

Date

Dear Dr. __________

My name is ________ and I am a state Licensed Acupuncturist who has recently opened my practice in _______. I wanted to touch base with you to give you a little information about myself and my practice. I am looking to connect with a local orthopedic specialist that I could refer patients to as well as offer my services for their patients that might be candidates for acupuncture. I appreciate how busy you must be so I will be very brief.

I recently graduated from ________ College and obtained my state license and National Certification. While I treat a variety of different conditions, I have specialized training in treating the pain associated with neuromusculoskeletal conditions, especially spinal and other joint pains. There has been much confusion over the role of acupuncture in treating these conditions. For example, recent studies in the U.S. and Germany have shown acupuncture to be nearly twice as effective as conventional care for chronic low back pain but also concluded that varying needle placement did not seem to affect outcomes. This has led some skeptics to conclude that acupuncture must work via the placebo effect even though previous animal studies prove otherwise.

I would be happy to discuss these studies or any questions you might have about the viability of acupuncture as a complement to conventional care if you have an interest. For now, I just wanted to let you know that while the mechanisms of acupuncture are proving confounding to researchers, its safety and effectiveness for treating chronic low back pain and other joint pathologies has led both the British government and the German insurance industries to accept acupuncture as valid, reimbursable therapy. I also want to assure you that I see acupuncture as a complement to orthopedic medical care. Acupuncture stimulates the body's intrinsic resources and while this is helpful in many instances of pain and inflammation, there are limits to the types of conditions it can successfully treat.

Please let me know if you would like any additional information and I very much appreciate your taking the time to read this letter.

Sincerely,

________, L.Ac.
(Name of practice)
(Address)
(Website)

Osteopaths:

Osteopaths are basically trained the same as medical doctors except that Osteopaths learn a system of bone and joint manipulation even though fewer and fewer of them practice this anymore. Being that Osteopaths were once viewed by the mainstream medical community as quacks they tend to be more sympathetic to other health care professions that have been marginalized by the mainstream. Although little separates today's Osteopaths and Medical Doctors in their methods of practice, many will tend to be more open to Holistic approaches including A/OM practitioners and, like Naturopaths, can make for good professional contacts.

Pain Management/Physical Medicine Physicians:

Pretty much everything I advise for approaching Orthopedic Physicians can be used or modified for Pain Management/Physical Medicine Physicians. The one additional wrinkle you might want to add with this group is that acupuncture has been shown to have some success with painful conditions that are thought be activated by spinal cord or perhaps even brain triggers. Pain authorities are finally figuring-out that just because a patient feels pain in a certain part of their body, it does not necessarily means the pain is being generated there. More and more, it is being postulated that the problem may be within pain signal relays such as in the spinal cord. I have yet to see authorities realize that these pain signals must also be interpreted by the brain so it must also be possible that when people feel pain in one part of the body, it could also be due to errant brain functioning. I predict they will one day realize this is also possible and may explain phenomena like phantom limb pain. Acupuncture has a chance to help some of these conditions although, based on the pattern of symptoms I detailed earlier, the odds of success may be low.

Pediatricians:

There are so many children's disorders that can be helped with A/OM but few parents or doctors ever consider this. It is my experience that children under 3-4 years of age respond especially well to the hands-on techniques of acupressure, massage, or tui-na and the numerous different methods to stimulate the skin. Babies' nervous systems are not fully developed when first born and that is why it is so important for babies to be held and stroked—this stimulation helps finish nature's job of building the neural connections needed for sending signals. I am not sure what those in our A/OM schools are learning about the specialized field of pediatrics in A/OM, but if you have the chance to study this it can help your chances of building a successful practice. This is also an area where learning herbs for children will greatly expand what you are able to do to help these patients. When moms find out you can help their children, they will love you and tell all their mommy friends. If you learn how to treat children and can get a Pediatrician to send you some patients, word will spread between the moms and you could find yourself very busy.

Physical Therapists:

Acupuncture is the perfect complement to physical therapy and every physical therapy facility should have an acupuncturist working together with the therapy staff. Until that happens, trying to connect with P.T's in your area is a very good idea. The new wrinkle here is that some states now allow Physical Therapists to perform what they call "dry needling." While this practice evolved from Trigger Point injection therapy, it is nothing more than needling ahshi points. So here you may need to do some homework to find-out if the P.T's in your area are doing dry needling but this tends to be less of an issue at this point in time than Chiropractors doing acupuncture in some states.

Urologists:

Acupuncture can sometimes be effective in treating urinary incontinence and the painful bladder condition of interstitial cystitis (I.C.) and most of these patients will be managed by—or at least seen by—urologists. Most urologists will not be aware that acupuncture could help urinary incontinence and few will think of acupuncture as a viable therapy for I.C. In my experience, acupuncture will help most women with urinary incontinence if they have not had surgery leading to the incontinence. Following surgery the odds decrease because the damage done may be beyond the body's resources to repair but it may still be worth a try. Please see my advice on a treatment protocol for this condition in my section on some of my favorite point combinations near the end of this book.

CHAPTER TWENTY

Getting Off To a Fast Start

As surviving the first few years is so important to building a successful practice, I wanted to offer some advice on how you can better your chances of getting off to a fast start. The advice I offer here is meant to supplement that given in the chapters on *Office Location*, *Getting Them in Your Door*, *Establishing your Fees*, *Accepting Insurance*, and so forth. As with the advice I offer throughout this book, the following are suggestions that should be helpful in most situations but are not the only ways practitioners can find success.

I strongly urge you to keep your overhead down. While there may be instances where spending more in the beginning will payoff, opening your practice is a gamble and it will be much safer if you learn the ropes by starting to gamble at the low-stakes table. As I mentioned in the Chapter Eighteen, I don't recommend you practice out of your house but rather find a professional looking office building. Doing so will likely mean that your office space expense will be the single biggest expense you will have. I also suggested in that chapter that an office of around 500-600 square feet should be good to start and that you should look to begin with a shorter term lease of 1-2 years with an option to renew. Finding a modestly-sized office in a good building and in a decent area of town with a relatively short beginning lease will greatly reduce the debt obligation you will be taking-on.

Another expense that can be a significant problem for establishing your practice is student loan debt. I mentioned in the beginning of this book that the NCCAOM's 2008 Job Training Analysis survey found that 50% of those who responded to the survey carried an average of

$40,000 in student loans. I have heard of other figures regarding graduates from some schools carrying twice that amount or even more. I really don't know what to tell those who have already run-up such debt other than to say that, if you are serious about making a career out of your practice, you are going to have to work that much harder to build your practice while paying off that debt. About the only advice I can offer those carrying high debt is to seriously research how to reduce your payments by finding other sources of loans. If you own a house with enough equity, would a home equity loan be at a lower rate than your student loan? Managing student loan debt is the sort of issue that a well-functioning State or National professional association should be able to help their members with.

For those in school who are not yet in deep debt, do everything you can to make it through school with as little debt as possible. It is not like there are high paying jobs waiting for you as soon as you graduate. If anything, the hard work is just beginning after you get licensed and the deeper in debt you are when you start your practice the more pressure you will be under to earn higher income that much sooner.

The next big expense I advise you to avoid is hiring any front office personnel such as a receptionist. As I mentioned earlier, in the first three years of my practice, I ran the whole thing by myself. Everything. I answered phones, set appointments, drove to Chinatown to buy my herbs, kept the office clean, you name it. This should be manageable because you will not be seeing many patients in the very beginning unless you get lucky. Once you get to the point that you are seeing 6-8 patients a day, you can then hire a part-time receptionist. My first receptionist was a patient of mine that thought what I was doing in my practice was great and wanted to help and did not care about making anything over minimum wage. If you have a spouse who can help that is even better but in my case my wife was full-time busy with our two children and again, my modest patient load those first 2-3 years made it feasible for me to run the whole show. As our children got older, my wife began working in our office and now she works three days a week as our office manager and we have another person working the other two days. It is true that finding good help that is affordable is a real problem but it should only be a problem once you are seeing enough patients and generating enough income that you really need to hire someone. Reaching that point means that you have made it through the most crucial beginning survival stage and are now into the problems that you face in the growth stages.

I know some will disagree with the above feeling that managing a one person practice might seem unprofessional and that people will be more impressed if you have a receptionist. You may also get the advice that when you only have a few patients a day you should schedule them close together so your patients will think you are busy. While I understand the thinking behind this approach, my advice is that you don't play games with your patients. You want to cultivate an honest, collaborative relationship with them. They will be impressed with your honesty, integrity, and most of all, the results you achieve for them. If anything, if they see you as being a skilled and professional caregiver that is struggling to build a humble practice and has few patients starting-out, they will be more likely to want to help you by referring others to you. It is fine to cluster your few patients a day near each other so the one coming in sees the one going out, but don't try to put on airs. Schedule your patients at the time they most want in order to make it easiest for them when you are just starting out and have the flexibility to do so. You might have to later re-train some of your first patients to no longer expect to be able to get in to see you whenever they want on short notice but this again is one of those nice problems you will have once you get through the survive or fail period and are into the growing the established practice phase.

In addition to keeping your overhead down, you should give a lot of thought to trying to line-up patients even before you open your practice. One way you can do this is to let all your friends, family and acquaintances know when you will be open for practice. Let them know what a big step and accomplishment this is, how difficult it can be to get started and ask them to help you by letting you help them with your services. You should especially try to find those who have some insurance coverage for acupuncture (verifying this by calling their insurance company before starting treatment) as this will allow them to get treated by you with little if any cost to them. You can't bill insurance for immediate family members, however. For those without any insurance coverage for acupuncture, offer them a discount. I don't suggest you offer treatments for free as this sends the wrong signal. Of course, you will give free treatments to very close friends or family, but in the outreach you do to notify your broadest circle of contacts, it is best for them to appreciate that you do have overhead costs and that there will be a fee for your services. When you make this outreach make sure you repeatedly ask your circle of contacts to please let their circle of contacts know about your new practice. Informing people in this way is exactly the kind of thing that social media resources such as Facebook or others can be very useful for. As acupuncture is still in such an early stage in the West, few of your friends will know anyone else who is an acupuncturist so you opening your practice should be an occasion that gets talked about within that circle. It is not like you are opening yet another Starbucks so take advantage of the fact that you are doing something unusual and very useful and try to build some buzz about it.

You should begin this process while still in school by sending regular updates on the types of patients you are seeing and helping in your internship and the patients helped in your school clinic in general. One of the most important lessons you need to learn to help you market your services is to appreciate that people don't understand all of the conditions acupuncture has the potential to help. They just don't get that acupuncture sparks the body's resources and that this has applications in virtually all conditions. Even those patients you were successful with that think you are the greatest won't automatically think to check with you about how you might be able to help some conditions. The more they hear about how you or any acupuncturist was successful helping this or that condition, the more they will think of you if they or someone they know has those conditions. In your communications with your circle of contacts, keep naming conditions helped by acupuncture and reminding them to please share this information and your contact information with everyone they know.

If you can get several friends and family to come to you when you first open—especially those with insurance coverage—this can make a huge difference in the first few months of your practice. You don't want to be paying your overhead with nothing coming in those first months. A good general goal can be to try to at least generate enough income to cover your rent within the first 1-2 months and then to cover your entire overhead within 3-6 months. If you can get a handful of family members and friends to let you treat them during those first months—starting at twice a week then reducing to once a week—this should allow you to meet those goals while you work your tail off doing all of the things I mentioned in the chapter *Getting Them In Your Door.*

Retirement Facilities:

When I first opened my office in San Dimas, California, I was unaware that there were several good retirement facilities in that area. Some of the first brave souls that let this young, inexperienced acupuncturist treat them were older patients in pretty poor condition. I had only treated a few of this type of patient in my internship and I was skeptical as to how they would respond to acupuncture considering their overall qi depleted state and that the conditions they were seeking help for were so chronic. I was surprised to learn that, kind of like treating children, many elderly patients just need a little nudge to make a big difference in their symptoms. Unlike children and many healthy adults, however, this nudge does not help them get over their problems completely but can make a big difference in the severity of their symptoms. Treating older patients is not only very rewarding, but word spreads very quickly in retirement facilities. Older patients were a big factor in my survival in my first years and have remained an important cornerstone of my practice's foundation over the years. I have done some teaching on treating the elderly and hope to do more so look for information on this at my website.

I highly recommend that you look into the retirement facilities in your area and ask about giving talks there. Some may even have their own little publications that would have inexpensive ads you could take out. Find a way to give a good discount to these patients as most are on very limited budgets (see Chapter Sixteen for more on this). When I say limited budgets, I mean some elderly patients will be deciding whether or not to get a treatment with you or pay other bills. Do everything you can to help these people. Many are struggling to live their last years with dignity and are really struggling with health issues. Being that you are not going to be super-busy in your first year or two, this is a great time to offer your services at low rates and help those who are struggling while building your practice. And don't forget that, if you build a good reputation as being effective and caring for this patient demographic, word will spread especially within the retirement facilities including to the caregivers who work there and the family members of those you help. That kind of word of mouth can make a huge difference in supporting your practice in the early stages.

One last bit of advice I want to give you about getting off to a fast start is to join and get involved with your student association at your school and to do the same in your state and national professional associations. I know—I know—I can hear the groans now. Getting involved with such groups may seem like the most boring waste of time you could imagine but you never know just what the contacts you make or the knowledge you gain might do for you in your career. I am going to go into more detail on this in the last chapter where I will give my take on the current state of the A/OM profession but I mention it here because what you can gain in becoming a member of such groups can be one more useful advantage in getting off to the best start possible.

CHAPTER TWENTY-ONE

Turning Failure into Success

The advice I will be offering here could apply to both helping you get off to a fast start and to growing your practice over the years because it is fundamental to all stages of practice. I mentioned in the first chapter that no one heals everybody and that you will have your failures with patients no matter how skilled you may get. I also stated that your patient satisfaction rate should be higher than your "success" rate with specific problems. What I was getting at with that way of putting things is that your goal should be to provide everyone who walks in your door with a valuable service even if you are not able to help them for the problem they came to you for. Because acupuncture stimulates the body's own healing resources and we seldom get 100% of those resources, a well trained acupuncturist should always be able to give most everyone a boost to their self-healing/managing system. This being the case, everyone you treat should be able to get at least a little something positive out of your treatment.

More important than the general boost acupuncture should consistently give everyone treated with the method, however, is that you should always look to see if there are any other health issues your patients have in addition to the one(s) that brought them to you. You may end up not being able to help a patient's neck pain, for example, but you might very well be able to help their sinus congestion problem. Now, they may tell you that they don't really care about their sinus problem and that they are only seeing you to get help for their neck pain. But, while you should of course make the neck pain your number one priority, you should look to add some points or prescribe some herbs (if they will take them) for their additional problem of sinus congestion. Most everyone has more than one health issue so finding out about any additional ones should be done as early into the treatment process as possible. Your intake form should have given them the opportunity to give information on all body systems but, if they didn't mark anything other than the main complaint, ask them during your intake process if they have any other issues they might like help for.

Just how you go about learning of and adding for additional problems can vary based on the details of each individual and your style of practice. You just want to do all you can to see that every patient gets something positive out of their interaction with you. That can also include you referring them to someone better suited to help them. Telling a patient that you are sorry but you are afraid you just are not going to be able to help their problem is never fun but it is a reality of practice. Remember I said in the first chapter that the best of the best probably only help 80%-85% of their patients? That means a great Master seeing 10 patients a day will have 2 people on average they will have failed to help each of those days. By learning how to discover and treat additional problems, you can't reduce the number of patients whose main problem you were unable to help, but you can reduce the number of patients you were unable to help at all.

Learning how to reduce the number of patients you could not help at all not only makes it easier on you by not having to have as many awkward conversations explaining the treatment is not working and not going to work, it also increases patient satisfaction rates, keeps those patients coming to you for more treatment, and increases the number of referrals those patients will generate over time.

CHAPTER TWENTY-TWO

Growing Your Practice Over the Years

A major theme of this book has been focusing on how to survive the first few years of practice. In this chapter I want to offer advice on how to grow your practice from the foundation you established in those first years. When I say "grow" your practice, I am not referring to offering advice on how to establish a large clinic with many others working under you. I have no experience with this as I decided in my first years that I would keep my practice a very simple one with low overhead and allowing me to support my family while also giving me the flexibility to pursue other projects related to spreading A/OM to the public. As I get closer to retirement age, I may look to build that multi-practitioner center I first envisioned when I opened my initial practice and called it the "Holistic Care Center" as this would allow me to generate some passive income. If I ever go down that road and learn how to do this, I would be happy to share that information. For now, the advice I will be offering here is about growing your practice to a higher volume and higher profit solo-practice.

I mentioned in the first chapter that once you build your patient base (of satisfied patients), growing your practice becomes easier. This is due to the increased number of repeat patient visits and the growing number of past patients who refer others to you. This phenomenon of exponential growth over time is the reward for doing things right in your first years but like everything else about practice building, it must be nurtured to maximize its potential. I cannot express strongly enough how even your most supportive patients will tend to not understand all you have the potential to do for them or their friends. I stressed in earlier chapters how you can start to address this by emphasizing that acupuncture stimulates one's natural resources. No matter how much you stress this with each of your patients in the beginning of their treatment process, you can greatly help the growth of your practice over the years by reminding your past patients of this fact.

You should develop a patient database from the very start of your practice that at least contains the patient's name, contact information, and the last time they were seen by you. You should capture the contact information you need on your patient intake form. It is especially useful to get an email address as then you can send your correspondences at no cost. Not everyone will have email of course so you will want to do a mixed mailing of emails and regular snail mail and then keep your database current when returns indicate the address is no longer valid. You will then want to send out some sort of correspondence to those patients on a regular basis. One way to do this is to send out a simple newsletter perhaps quarterly. As I mentioned in Chapter Twenty, you should make sure you discuss some cases that you helped. Nothing impresses people more and helps them understand the potential of your services better than describing how you helped someone with a specific condition. You may want to highlight how A/OM can help a specific condition with each newsletter. You can also reference recent scientific studies that have been published showing acupuncture having a positive effect on some specific condition. Your newsletter would also be a great place to highlight any classes you are offering as I suggested in the cross-marketing section in Chapter Nineteen.

A good format for a regular newsletter then would be to have general information describing a certain condition, describe how you helped a patient with that condition, include that patient's short testimonial, cite some published research, and then give helpful hints about elements of self-care people with that condition should follow. You can then have a notice for and description of any classes you are offering and always make sure you let them know how grateful you are for their referrals.

While a newsletter is a great marketing resource, there are many other types of notices you can send people in your database. You can send birthday cards or notices about new herbal products, etc. The important thing is to reach-out to your former patients a few times a year. This is so important to growing your practice because people will forget about you and getting anything that reminds them of you will often spur them to contact you for an appointment. As with any good practice, you can overdo these types of notifications. You don't want to be sending out these types of things every week or even every month as that would be overkill. Another important benefit about maintaining an updated database of your patients' contact information is that having this will make your practice much more valuable if you should ever look to sell your practice.

In addition to touching base with your former patients on a regular basis, you should also do this with the health and wellness professionals you have been cultivating for referrals over the years. You should always send them a note (email or snail mail) thanking them for any referral they gave you and when appropriate giving them an update on the patient they referred. But it is also a good idea to send some sort of periodic correspondence like a Happy New Year's notice or if you have added classes that might be relevant to the types of patients they send you, etc. As with your patients, you just want to drop them some sort of line that reminds them about you and your services. Don't go overboard on this, twice a year would be plenty.

CHAPTER TWENTY-THREE

Some of My Favorite Point Combinations

First, let me state what should be so obvious it could go unsaid but I better say it anyway: There are always exceptions to any general rule. The point combinations I offer here have helped me help thousands of patients over the years but no simple set of point combinations will be the best way to go in any given case. I firmly believe, however, that employing some tried and true combinations together with what I have taught you about how to manage your patients within the private practice setting will often get as good if not better results than a "superior" individually tailored treatment done without understanding how to manage patients.

Neuromusculoskeletal Pain in General:

My specialty is using local points found by palpation. Practice your palpation techniques for goodness sake. Nothing will serve you better in your career. I didn't start out relying on local points but I later learned how to make them work for me better than using different strategies for distal/associated points. This being the case, local points are usually my Plan A. I also like to use opposite points in cases involving pain. Palpate the exact epicenter of the pain as best you can and needle the exact opposite point. Opposite points are easy to understand on problem spots in the extremities—a pain in the left Liver 8 spot can be needled at the right Liver 8 spot. Opposite points are not so easy on the torso or head but just visualize an arrow going straight through the problem spot on through the middle space and out again. Where the arrow would come out again is where to apply acupuncture or acupressure. Opposite points are often my Plan B. If I am not happy with how Plan A is working after 2-4 treatments (carefully monitoring as I taught you to do), I will switch to Plan B.

Some will say that using local points can make the symptoms flair-up. That is usually only the case when you needle too aggressively such as any combination of too deep, with a larger gauge needle or strong stimulating technique. Some people though, will get a little flair-up of their pain even with superficial needling and gentle manipulation techniques. These people usually do very well with opposite points. Once they are at least 50% better using opposite points, you can then do local points to finish the job. If you are using local points as your Plan A and seeing even 10% of your patients having flair-ups with the first treatment or two, you are doing something wrong and should go ahead and use opposite points as your Plan A until you learn how to be more subtle in your needle techniques.

I almost never use local or opposite points alone but mix them with other points geared to address underlying considerations. Local or opposite points used for any muscle/tendon problem can be supplemented with GB34, for example. A local point for abdominal pain can be supplemented with ST36 and so on.

Low Back Pain:

Local Points:

A great combination of points for lumbar pain is GV4, the extra GV point below the 4th lumbar vertebra (let's call this GV3 ½), and GV3 and then BL23, BL24, and BL25. You can then supplement this with GB34 and BL40.

If there is pain toward the hip or posterior superior Iliac crest (PSIS), you can add GB29 or better yet palpate ahshi points and needle those.

If there is pain and/or numbness radiating down the leg, note which meridian it is on or closest to and use points on those. For sciatica or Bladder meridian pain, you can add BL36 or BL37 as well as BL40. I tend to rely more on the combination of BL37 and then BL39 or BL40.

I may also add BL58 if the pain and/or numbness goes into the lower leg. The prone position is best for this treatment.

If there is pain down the side of the leg near the GB meridian use GB30, GB31, GB34, and then GB39 if into the lower leg. If this pain down the side of the leg is unilateral (as it usually is) I will often treat with the patient lying on their "good" side (lateral recumbent position).

Pain and/or numbness radiating in the front of the thigh is usually the most difficult to treat. For this you may want to do both the opposite points in the lower abdomen (explained next) as well as the local lumbar points or rotate between these two (local/opposite) on alternate treatments. When treating lower abdominal points, you can then add some local points in the thigh but be aware of the arteries/nerves there.

Opposite Points:

You can and should palpate for ahshi points in the lower abdomen but a good formula of points would be CV4, CV5, CV6, ST27, and ST28. To these it is very helpful to add SP6 and GB34. I also usually add SP9. I use SP6 and SP9 on at least 75% of those I treat in the supine (face-up) position as I will explain later. I will also often add LI 11 as a means to balance the upper with the lower and then also add auricular (ear) points Lumbar spine and Shenmen.

Review:

Low back pain:

Local points – GV4, GV3 ½, GV3, BL23, BL24, BL25, BL40 and then add GB34.

Opposite Points: CV6, CV5, CV4 and ST27, ST28, SP6, and GB34

With pain and/or numbness radiating in the BL channel (sciatica):

Add BL36, BL37, and BL58 to the above local points.

With pain and/or numbness radiating down the GB meridian:

Add GB30, GB31, GB34, and GB39 to the effected side to the local low back pain combination.

With pain and/or numbness radiating down the front of the thigh:

Treat using opposite points CV6, CV5, CV4, ST27, ST28 and GB34 then palpate and needle local thigh points being mindful of arteries and nerves.

Knee pain:

A great combination is bi-lateral ST34, ST35, SP10, Inner Knee Eye extra point, SP9, and LV8. When you needle the two "eyes" of the knee—ST35 and the Inner Knee Eye (we could call this SP 9 ½)—point the tip of the needle toward the middle of the knee cap and insert 1 to 1 ½ inch (carefully, of course). You can then add LI11 or better yet, palpate the central sore spot in the knee and then needle the spot on the elbow that most mirrors the knee sore spot. If you don't know how to do this type of mirroring technique – see my book *The Healing Power of Acupressure and Acupuncture Chapter Ten—Treating Common Health Problems*. You can also add auricular points Shenmen and the Knee point.

Shoulder, wrist, or ankle pain:

Palpate or otherwise ascertain the epicenter of the pain and, if it is on or near a meridian, needle other nearby points on that meridian in addition to the ahshi point itself. For a point at or near LI 15, for example, add LI14, LI13, and LI11. Also add SP6 and GB34 and auricular points Shenmen and the opposite point that corresponds to the ahshi point. Use these points bi-laterally.

Hip pain:

Bi-lateral GB30, GB31, GB34, GB39 and palpate and needle ahshi points then add SP6, SP9 and auricular points Shenmen and Hip.

Reproductive hormone balance, general balance tune-up:

We live in a yang dominated society in which yin deficiency is epidemic. A great combination of points to help counter this is:

Bi-lateral SP6, SP9, CV4, CV5, ST27, ST28 and auricular Shenmen. To this you can also add CV12, CV17 and GV20 to balance the middle and upper aspects. This is a beautiful formula, good for dozens of disorders.

Sinus problems including sinus headaches:

Bi-lateral GB14 and ST3. This powerful combination will usually begin to clear sinus congestion within 10 minutes of insertion although this may only last a short while after the patient is upright again. Even if that happens, getting just temporary sinus clearing is a good sign that the treatment will have a positive affect the next day or two and even better with a series of treatments. As well as these or other points can work for sinus problems, Chinese herbs work even better and they are very inexpensive. Two of the best patent formulas for sinus problems are Pe Min Kan Wan and Bi-Yan.

It is a good idea to add bi-lateral SP6 and LU5 or LU7 to the above two sets of points as this will help make for a more broad balancing treatment. When needling GB14, pay attention to how the needles will tend to flop one way or another because there is so little flesh to needle into. The lighter, plastic handled needles are better than the heavier metal-wrapped handled needles for this point as well as other facial points. GB14 is also very useful in hormone balancing in my experience as well as GB21 as they seem to have an effect on balancing the ovaries/testis.

Urinary incontinence:

As most cases of non-surgically caused incontinence are due to weakness in rising (yang) qi, points in the upper part of the body such as scalp points and especially GV 20 can help this. A good formula of points is to use CV3, CV4, CV9, Bi-lateral ST 30, ST29, LI11, then

GV20 and bi-lateral auricular points Bladder and Shenmen points. Start with CV3 as the first point inserted and GV20 as the last point inserted and then remove in the same order with GV20 being the last point removed. You need to use a stronger stimulation on GV20 as this makes the upward qi attraction stronger. It is also crucial to stress to your patients that they need to practice Kegel exercises regularly. Many patients will have improvement within the first treatment or two and be thrilled but if they don't keep-up the Kegel exercises, the incontinence will often return.

CHAPTER TWENTY-FOUR

My Take on the State of the Profession

I wanted to offer my thoughts on where I see the A/OM profession in the U.S. at this point in time because I believe no book on practice building could be comprehensive without considering this. Like all else in this book, the following is my opinion based on my experiences over my more than 25 years in practice and my time as a student. Like it or not, there are important reasons why anyone getting started in this field should try to become familiar with the issues affecting the profession as a whole. I am not saying no one can become successful in practice without this understanding but having some knowledge of these profession-wide issues will help, especially if you follow my advice on how your involvement can greatly improve your odds of success. Please indulge me while I cover some ancient history, I promise this will lead to some useful advice.

I first became involved in "acu-politics" while still a student. One of my teachers helped develop the NCCA (before it became the NCCAOM). He explained to me the idea was to establish an exam that would meet professional certification/licensing standards so that it would be easier to get individual states to legalize acupuncturists by giving states the opportunity to use this exam instead of spending the time and money to develop their own entry-level licensing exams. While I did not work on this myself, I followed the progress of this effort over the years getting to know and having a lot of respect for those who made it happen. It was a good idea and due to the years of hard work that was put into this effort, the rate at which states passed legislation legalizing acupuncturists was much faster than it would have been and this effort increased the credibility of our profession's standards.

During the time I was in school, my state of California had already passed legislation establishing a committee to oversee our certification including developing and administering the state exam and approving schools. This being the case, the NCCA exam development was not followed too closely here. Most of the people in California involved in acu-politics were working on improving our status in this state and not so much in national acu-politics. While I tried to follow what was happening on the national stage, I first got involved in California acu-politics as a student when legislation was being promoted that would have mandated health insurance companies cover acupuncture. I attended meetings at an acupuncture school where those fighting for this held strategy sessions. This legislation did eventually pass but only after changing the wording in it from stating insurance companies would "provide" coverage to "offer" coverage. While a somewhat hollow victory, passing this legislation was a victory and some of those who got together to work on this decided it would be a waste to disband so they formed a professional association—the California Acupuncture Association or CAA.

I did not join the leadership of the CAA until a couple of years later and spent a few years chairing a committee and serving on their Executive Committee and their Board of Directors. At one point during this time, the leadership of the AAAOM asked to have a meeting with the CAA leadership. The CAA had grown quite quickly and had done a good job of building the infrastructure of a well functioning professional association. The AAAOM leadership asked for the meeting to plead with us to join forces with them as they were burning out running from state to state trying to get legislation passed to legalize acupuncturists in as many states as possible. To my surprise, the leadership of the CAA declined the invitation and this, in my opinion, drove a wedge between national and California acu-politics that has still not been completely resolved today. As California has the largest number of A/OM practitioners (around 40% of the nation's total), this lack of cooperation between those working on a national level and California has hindered our profession's growth.

During the period just following the CAA's decision to not team-up with the AAAOM, the California and national groups did their own thing with little communication between them. In addition to the NCCAOM and AAAOM, two other important "national" organizations were further developed; the body that sets curriculum standards and accredits A/OM schools (ACAOM) and the organization of representatives of those schools (CCAOM). The development of these organizations established the foundation of the A/OM profession's primary infrastructure: A national professional association (AAAOM), an exam/certification system (NCCAOM), a school and curriculum accreditation body (ACAOM), and a coalition of school representatives (CCAOM).

These four bodies have all played important roles in advancing the A/OM profession in the U.S. and each of these organizations have an interest in seeing this growth continue and improve. But, while there are shared interests between these groups in the growth of the A/OM profession, there is also—or at least should be—a natural check and balance dynamic. What is best for one of these groups is not always best for another. This is how it should be. These groups need to keep their missions firmly in mind for them to meet those missions and to maintain their credibility. Looking for and working on common goals is of course a good thing, but there should occasionally be natural disagreements and cross-purposes between these groups. A healthy check and balance system is best for both the profession and the public.

Unfortunately, one of these four groups has for many years now been unhealthy and unable to serve its function in this check and balance system. This is our professional associations—both on the national level and, for the most part, at the state levels. This weakness has festered despite the best attempts and very hard work put-in by many who served in leaderships roles of these organizations. Something different must be done to improve the health of our professional associations. I believe there is a solution and the reason I am sharing this with you in a book on practice building is because those of you coming out of school or already in practice can not only fix this problem but, in doing so, you can greatly increase your chances of building a successful practice. So, not only can you provide a service to the profession, you can do a great deal to help yourself at the same time.

I mentioned in the first chapter that there have been different opinions over the years about what adjustments are needed to help the growth of the A/OM profession and improve the odds of success of those entering this field. A major theme of this book has been my view that the key to making a living offering acupuncture services is learning how to properly value those services within their respective markets. I also mentioned that my view on this was a recent refinement of my previous view that the key to practice success was educating the public about acupuncture services and Licensed Acupuncturists. While my refined belief regarding this came from my realization that a good number of acupuncturists all over the world are struggling to make a living, I still believe quite strongly that, in the U.S. at this point in time, public education is badly needed to improve the odds of success in this field.

The history I offered above regarding the development of the A/OM profession's primary infrastructure is a brief overview of the development of a profession that is new to the West. Many of the early supporters of A/OM in the U.S. were firmly convinced that acupuncture was destined to be accepted as a valuable healing resource and to their credit and the benefit of us all they set about building the infrastructure that would facilitate this acceptance. During those early years it was only natural that most of the emphasis was placed on promoting legislation to legalize acupuncturists while establishing our schools and exam systems. The focus during this stage then was essentially top-down—working with legislatures and other policy makers to establish those offering acupuncture services as a regulated profession meeting established standards.

The problem was that once we had acupuncturists legal in most states and had our school accreditation and exam systems in place, our professional associations should have shifted their focus away from supporting those efforts and toward educating the public about acupuncture and acupuncturists. This shift in priorities never took place. We spent all these years fighting those who opposed us and building a brand new profession to service the public, but we never got around to educating the public about who we are and what we do! There were some modest, short term attempts at this, but nothing ever approaching the level of effort that went into building our infrastructure. It makes no sense at all that a group would go through the trouble to build a brand new profession and then do virtually nothing to announce to the public that this profession stands ready to serve them.

I have my theories why this shift in priorities never took place but those are not important now. What matters now is that we need those entering this field to take the lead in shifting those priorities. I keep using the term "public education" but this could also be called "marketing."

Some people seem uncomfortable with the idea of marketing as that sounds like advertising and of questionable ethics. We need to get over this attitude. Educating the public about acupuncture's potential and the training of Licensed Acupuncturists is a public service and absolutely ethical. It will also help more than anything else we can do to increase the number of those seeking our services.

The public is very curious and interested in acupuncture but they are afraid to try to seek it out without knowing anything about the type of people who perform acupuncture or just how the treatment will take place. I explained in the Chapter Nineteen how the public's lack of understanding about Licensed Acupuncturists makes it imperative that we portray ourselves as caring, intelligent professionals. In that chapter, I offered ideas on how you can do that yourself in your own market but I mentioned that we also need to work on this within the profession as a whole. This is what needs to become the top priority of our professional associations and those entering this profession can make that happen.

Over the last 20 years, our various state and national associations have spent hundreds of thousands if not millions of dollars collectively on the top-down efforts especially lobbying for different legislation. This was needed in the past but now we need to raise money and human resources for public education/marketing. There are many ways we can reach out to educate the public about who we are and what we do. It does not have to take huge sums of money to make great progress. There are many cost-effective ways to do this if we get creative, especially in this age of information technology.

Doing so will not only help the A/OM profession to become better understood by the public but will also help us to secure our place as the acupuncturists with the greatest degree of training. Over the last 30 years many different health care professions have worked at getting acupuncture within their scope of practice. Medical Doctors can practice acupuncture in most states without undergoing any required training, Chiropractors can practice acupuncture in many states with 200 hours of training or even less and now Physical Therapists are needling ahshi points and calling it Dry Needling. Up until now, most of the leaders in the A/OM profession have tried to slow or stop this by stressing that these other professions should not be allowed to practice acupuncture with so little training but this approach has not been effective in most instances. Instead of relying on appealing to regulators to stop other health care professionals from practicing acupuncture, the A/OM profession should instead reach-out to the public and make our case there.

When we spend our meager resources trying to lobby regulators asking them to prevent other health care professionals from practicing acupuncture, we usually fail. But, even when we are successful, we still create bad blood between fellow health care professionals we could be working together with for the public good. If we were to shift our focus to educating the public about how our training standards in acupuncture are the most rigorous, we take the high road, don't insult other health care professionals, and would always end up with the badly needed positive effect of educating the public about our profession. This would help to both increase our profession's patient base while protecting our future by solidifying ourselves as the top authorities in A/OM. Better to go on the offensive of building our standing with the public rather than trying to tear others down.

What Is Needed Now

What you can do to make public education a priority is to join the AAAOM as a student member if you are still a student or a professional member if you are licensed and INSIST THAT THEY MAKE PUBLIC EDUCATION PRIORITY NUMBER ONE. Show your support for this by both your membership and by offering to pay extra for a public education fund. You should also do the same with your state association. There has been some 30,000 acupuncture licenses/certificate issued in the U.S. No one seems to know exactly how many are practicing right now but there are many thousands out there, many of them are struggling and we, as a profession, are doing NO MARKETING! There are also about 8,000 students enrolled in some 60 A/OM colleges at any given time. All we need is for a reasonable number of those involved with this profession to contribute a regular modest sum to mount a very effective public education/marketing campaign. There could be no better way to invest in the future growth of the profession and individual practices.

What I am talking about here is banding together to mount a collective public education/marketing campaign. There is tremendous strength in numbers and we have the numbers to make great things happen. If between the schools, practitioners and merchant suppliers we could get just 2,000 to contribute $100 a month, we could mount a $200,000 a month campaign! This could involve print media, radio, producing documentaries, and much more. There is so much that could be done that would lift this profession from the margins to being a household word. The interest is there. People are fascinated by acupuncture and they are sick and tired of having drugs shoved down their throats every time they go to a doctor. They just need to have their fear of the unknown eased by educating them about how they can find intelligent, caring professionals to provide acupuncture services in a manner that reflects the value of this service.

There would of course be many details to work out but having the financing and people to help facilitate this will give us the means to address those details. With the economy in the shape it is in right now, professional help can be had for less money than was the case in the past. We could afford to hire some experienced professional to help us especially considering that some of them have been helped by acupuncture and would be willing to help us in our goal of spreading the good news to the public. Have you seen the documentary *9000 Needles*? It is a powerful movie about how A/OM helped turn an impending personal tragedy into a life of hope. This award winning movie is doing more to educate people about acupuncture than you could imagine. I have been working with that movie's director (the brother of the movie's subject) and he is open to making another documentary about A/OM that would even better educate the public. There are also many celebrities who have been helped by A/OM and we could get their help also. We just need to raise the funds to give us stable resources so we could mount a multi-year, multi-pronged campaign. If all we get is 1,000 contributing $50 a month, that is still $50,000 a month! We can do this.

All of you just entering practice or already in practice are going to have to spend thousands of dollars to begin and run your service business. I have tried to share with you my knowledge from years of my own successful practice to give you the best chance of becoming successful. As much as I believe the information I have shared will better your odds of making a success of your practice, I cannot stress enough how much better your odds will be if you band together with others like yourself and pool your resources into the type of campaign I describe above. I go through the trouble to tell you all this for your own good. My practice is very stable and I am in the final stretch toward my retirement (at least that is what I tell my wife). I have nothing to gain from this campaign. You have everything to gain and so do the millions of people you can help educate about A/OM. I will do everything I can to help make this happen if you step-up. I have been waiting for this for many years now.

Now that we have the infrastructure of our profession up and running, it is time to shift from the top-down approach of working with policymakers and put more emphasis on a bottoms-up approach of reaching-out directly to those we seek to service—the public. Our professional associations are the place to make this happen. They are the place where professionals gather to further the profession. We need fresh blood in these associations; people new to the profession who understand their best chance to earn a living is in private practice but also realize the power of collective marketing. The public is very interested in acupuncture but they know nothing about acupuncturists. You need to associate with your fellow professionals and educate the public. If you don't do it, no one will.

I hope you have found my advice helpful and I will do all I can to help you from here. Please give serious thought to what I have proposed in this chapter. Undertaking a collective marketing campaign together with employing the advice I have offered in this book should give you a good chance to enjoy the blessing of earning a comfortable living while helping others as I have. Thanks for taking the time to digest my advice and good luck.

Some Thoughts on my First Book

Early into this book, I briefly mentioned my first book; *The Healing Power of Acupressure and Acupuncture; A Complete Guide to Timeless Traditions and Modern Practice*. I wanted to take this opportunity to say a few things about that book as I believe it could be useful to A/OM students although in a very different manner than *Making Acupuncture Pay*. While *Making Acupuncture Pay* strives to offer concrete, practical advice on the nuts-and-bolts of private practice, *The Healing Power* book delves into A/OM history, philosophy, and theory.

Anyone practicing acupuncture will be asked many times how acupuncture was first discovered. No one knows the answer to this and I have long felt the inability to answer this question hurts acupuncture's credibility. I wanted to address this question because I thought I could offer a reasonable theory based on some of the Taoist folk legends I began to study in 1978 together with my experience as a practitioner. I also thought those legends offered important clues as to the origins of the fundamental concepts behind traditional Chinese thought such as yin/yang, qi, the Five Elements, and others. While I by no means claim to have solved the mystery behind the origins of these things, I like to think I was able to offer a reasonable set of theories for how they may have first began.

Although *The Healing Power* book was written for the general public, I hoped it would be seen as offering something useful to those in the A/OM profession as well. It took me several years to write and frankly it took a lot out of me and the growth of my practice. It then became difficult for me to find the time and energy to promote it to the A/OM profession. I mention this here because others have told me how much it helped them put the traditional theories into perspective. Not everyone will find the subject matter so practical but if you ever wondered how acupuncture and the theories behind Chinese medicine originally began my first book may help you to ponder this mystery.

CPSIA information can be obtained at www.ICGtesting.com
Printed in the USA
BVOW06s1618030116

431638BV00002B/99/P